I0644384

Routledge Revivals

Architecture and the Environment

First published in 1976, *Architecture and the Environment* is based on the authors very successful book Architecture of Children. The original book has been completely revised and new illustrations have been specially drawn. This book gives a comprehensive account of the role of architecture in the environment of a constantly developing world. It traces the history of building from its most primitive origins to the complex architecture of the current times. The book takes as a starting- point ideas that will be familiar to all its readers, then leads them on to an examination of the attitudes and approaches of architects and planners, so that they can follow the creative process step by step. The style of the book is direct and very readable, with a minimum of technological language and will be useful for general readers interested in architecture.

Architecture and the Environment

Maxwell Fry and Jane Drew

Routledge
Taylor & Francis Group

First published in 1976
by George Allen & Unwin Ltd.

This edition first published in 2023 by Routledge
4 Park Square, Milton Park, Abingdon, Oxon, OX14 4RN

and by Routledge
605 Third Avenue, New York, NY 10017

Routledge is an imprint of the Taylor & Francis Group, an informa business

A Library of Congress record exists under ISBN: 0047200200

ISBN: 978-1-032-61545-5 (hbk)
ISBN: 978-1-032-61550-9 (ebk)
ISBN: 978-1-032-61548-6 (pbk)

Book DOI 10.4324/9781032615509

Architecture and the Environment

Maxwell Fry and Jane Drew

London George Allen & Unwin Ltd
Ruskin House Museum Street

First published in 1976

ISBN 0 04 720020 0

Printed in Great Britain
in 11 point Baskerville type by
Cox & Wyman Ltd,
London, Fakenham and Reading

Acknowledgements

We are grateful to Josephine Crickmay for her work on the line drawings, to Michael Reynolds for the drawing of the Parthenon, and to the following for permission to reproduce illustrations: Aerofilms Ltd, 2, 30, 31, 32, 55, 61; Architectural Press, 61; Bellwood Photography Ltd, 62; BOAC, 50; Cement and Concrete Association, 42, 48; Civic Trust Photographic Library, 4, 23; G. Candilis, 60; Commission for the New Towns (Hemel Hempstead), cover; Department of the Environment, 71, 77, 78, 80; *Evening Standard* and John W. Benson, 56; Fry, Drew, Knight & Creamer, 51; Greater London Council, 25, 49; Hertfordshire County Council, 53; Kawasumi Architectural Photograph Office, 59; M. W. Keen (Commercial) Ltd, 45; Lennart af Petersens, 22; National Tourist Organisation of Greece, 66; National Trust, 3; Pilkington Brothers Ltd, 44; Radio Times Hulton Picture Library, 54; Royal Commission on Historical Monuments (England), 76; Runcorn Development Corporation, 57, 58; Sanders & Forster Ltd, 41; Studio Jaanus Ltd, 46; West Riding County Council, 43; A. D. Wood, 38.

Contents

Illustrations

I
Environment in a Changing World

This book is about architecture; what it is, what it came from and where, perhaps, it is going. It will tell you how buildings were made in the past and how they are made today, and will look at the long history of architecture from the very earliest days.

But you live in the present and in a world that is changing very fast, and so before we begin the long story of architecture we must tell you something of what is going on now, bringing in a good deal of the surroundings, the background and setting of architecture which are commonly called the *environment*.

In the earlier edition of this book, we tried never to see architecture as separate from its surroundings, but in the interval between the first writing of the book at the end of the last war and now we have all become very aware of three major aspects of change: first the increase in population, second the speed of all forms of communication, and third the speed of production of goods of all kinds by machines.

We feel the effect of these rapid changes in many ways. Our little group of islands is already overcrowded. Wherever you go there are people – the shops and supermarkets burst with people, the roads are jammed with cars; there are not enough houses and schools to go round; and everyone seems to be on the move, some of us pouring out of the country for business and holidays, others pouring into our country as tourists.

As if this were not enough we face further increases of population before the end of the century. The population of the United Kingdom is already more than 55 millions. By the end of the century we may exceed 68 millions.

These increases in population mean more dwellings, schools, shops, more roads, more food and goods; more of everything.

We have built over thirty new towns, villages have been expanded into little towns, and we have experimented with various forms of high density housing, some of which we regret. The new towns we have built are much better than the old ones that were not planned but only 'happened', as it were, but we have to do much more than this to keep up with the increase in the number of people, and, more important, we must do it well. The task of making the new environment worth living in is a great and challenging one.

The rapid increase in the speed of travel,

1 Wherever you go there are people with their wants and needs. We must learn how to fit us all into a changing world.

communication and movements of all sorts adds to our difficulties. If people stayed reasonably still one could deal with them. But the opposite is the case. London, for example, is not only a great city; it is also a vast movement of people, with millions coming in and millions going out every day. And whilst London is the chief magnet it is not alone, for everywhere else in the country there is a ceaseless coming and going of people and goods, by rail, road and air. And as in England so also in every country of the developed world. The first great increase of population in the nineteenth century was carried by the railways which did dreadful damage to our old towns, cutting through well-planned districts and swallowing up huge areas for goods yards. The new increase is carried by motor-cars and aeroplanes which use even more land and cut up our streets, squares and open spaces and fill the air with noise. Then just as railways occupied acres of land, so airfields require square miles of country that is needed for farming, or recreation, and between the airfield and the city it serves we have to construct motorways to bring numerous passengers and goods to and fro.

2 New forms of transport eat up the precious land and endanger our way of life in towns and country.

During the past few years we have become aware not only of these trends and the changes they have brought, but also of their side-effects. An American scientist–writer, Rachel Carson, was one of the first to draw attention to a situation that is the direct result of our over-activity. In order to provide enough for these great populations we have used our resources faster than we should. The precious soil that covers the earth so thinly, the oil, the minerals and metals that lie under it, the animal, bird and fish life that live off it – all these we have used faster than we can replace them – if they are replaceable at all.

Worse than this, we have frequently been careless and wasteful. If we in London use between fifty and sixty gallons of water per person per day, New York uses well over 100 gallons! We find it hard to deal with the quantity of rubbish people leave to be collected in London; in New York it is a nightmare.

But the rubbish of industry in the form of poisonous waste products, the sewage of great cities and the chemicals that are sprayed on the land to increase its fertility, are even greater problems. These find their way into lakes and rivers and from them to the seas and oceans to poison the small organisms upon which all fish feed, so that these great sources of food and life are being poisoned every day. Unless we all take action to prevent it and bring our world back into healthy balance we shall face disaster.

Rachel Carson in her book *The Seas Around Us*, which brought the world's attention to the situation, called this *pollution*, and people began to realise that pollution takes many forms; and all of them point to the waste and destruction of what we need to keep us alive and healthy. But this word also reminded us that nothing is really separate, and that whatever is done in one place has its effects on everything else, and everyone else; that we are in fact one great community in which each one of us is in some way responsible for everyone else.

In England we found some time ago that our city air was polluted with sulphur and other chemicals and a great load of dirt that hid the sun. London fog was as famous as California 'smog' has now become. Today a London fog is a rarity and the old 'pea-souper' is gone for ever thanks to the Clean Air regulations which we now willingly obey. The noise of cars and planes is more difficult to cope with. Much of the heavy traffic now goes on to the motorways, but our streets are still noisy, dangerous and full of fumes, while great areas of town and country suffer from the sound of the big jets.

Certainly we must bring pollution under control in this country first – charity begins at home, as the old saying has it. But since our rivers flow into the seas and oceans we must, in the end, collaborate with the rest of the world if the seas are to be made really healthy and fruitful again, and that is going to take time, patience and more goodwill

3 Beautiful buildings of the past are a national heritage that we must preserve: The Vyne, a mixture of styles with the first classical portico on an English country house.

4 A pedestrian precinct at Norwich.

than the world has shown in the past.

We in Britain can, however, take some credit for improving our environment, and ensuring that our world becomes a better place to live in. For example, there is the creation of *development areas*, where the Government uses subsidies to attract industry to places where the rate of employment has declined but where there is a plentiful supply of housing. The Government also makes grants to help people improve their houses where modern conveniences such as bathrooms or kitchens are lacking. Measures like these have been effective and help to improve the environment. There are other helpful laws such as the listing of certain buildings as 'historic', which means that these buildings cannot be pulled down or altered without permission. Many beautiful old buildings are maintained by the National Trust which also owns and administers areas of especially beautiful country and coastline. Most cities have parks and many villages and towns have 'commons' which are preserved by law. Furthermore, the whole country is protected in one way or another by planning schemes which are kept under constant observation in order to preserve both town and country in the best possible way, the one for housing or industry, the other for agriculture or recreation.

Much damage has been done in the past through greed, ignorance or plain carelessness and we hope that these mistakes will not be repeated. Since the beginning of this century when a small handful of reformers built the first garden cities at Letchworth and Welwyn, we have come to realise that architecture is not enough in itself, and that it must combine with all the elements of life that make up our total environment.

This is the goal we must all seek. As you read the book, and look back upon the long road that has led us to the present day, we hope that you will see more clearly how the goal may be reached and do your best to achieve it.

2 Building Needs

The History of Shelter

Man has built on the earth for a long time: the closer we look the farther back into time we trace the marks of his occupation.

During the course of thousands of years climates have changed, the ice has moved to and from the poles and wandering man has eked out an existence only when and where, by seeking shelter, he could gain some respite from the pressures of cold and wet, heat and dust, and from danger and starvation.

It is too cold for people to live out of doors all the time. There are men who spend most of their time in the open – sheep rangers, hunters, men who live lonely, single lives. They have their own means of keeping warm, and they live hard.

Whenever people take to settled ways of living, one of the first things they do is to look for some kind of a shelter from the cold, the rain and danger. Even the animals seek shelter. The birds have their nests, the lions their den, and even the sheep, who have to rely upon their thick wool coats to protect them from the weather, find some nook or cranny in which they may crouch when the blizzard blows across the mountain. They die in their hundreds during a hard winter, unless the farmer builds them a shelter of wattle or straw, or goes over the mountain to find them where they lie buried in the drifts. Sheep were never renowned for sense.

Curiously enough it is not always the big, strong, animals that survive the struggle for existence that has always gone on in the world, not the fierce, well-armed creatures with few rivals, but the small defenceless 'sat-on' animals, who, hunted and chivvied from pillar to post have had to think one stage ahead of their enemies or perish.

We have always come in the lowest class so far as fur, feathers, tusks, teeth and claws are concerned. We have no woolly coat. We are defenceless against cold. As soon as we stop working or moving we must shelter. Some kind of a dwelling is a grim necessity. Fortunately we have a brain. That – whenever we choose to use it – is where we score over the rest.

You can imagine how eagerly the members of the tribes that wandered over the face of Europe in the days before history was written, seized on the limestone caves they found in various parts, and how pleased they must have been with these first human dwellings. They must have felt settled and secure there to judge by the decorations they left on the walls.

But caves are rare finds, and we need not think about them further, except to note that most of the good caves in Europe and the East are still occupied by people who can't pay the rent of a house or who find a cave safer than a house in the present circumstances.

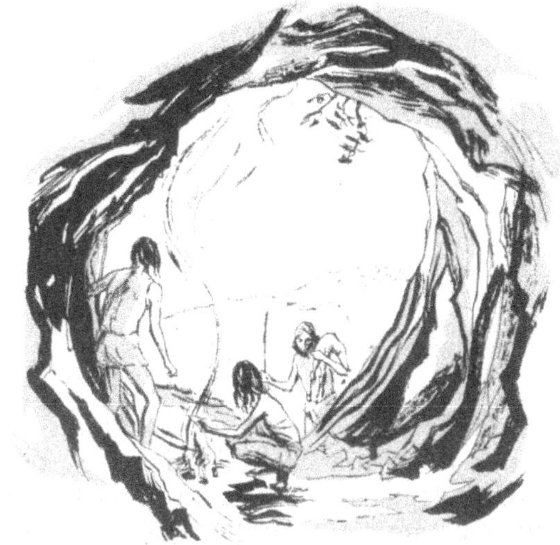

5 The cave offered the earliest protection for a settled life.

Those who could not find caves, and they were the majority, spent a lot of time building shelters for themselves, with whatever they could find that would do the job. For hundreds of years, for thousands of years, the search went on in every part of the world where man wandered or settled. The more settled he became in his habits, the more animals he collected round him; the more numerous his family grew – then the better his dwelling had to be.

What was it he wanted for his dwelling? What were his principal worries? It is not difficult to guess. You may think that you are very superior to the hairy savage who lived 2,000 years ago, but when your father is finding a new house for you to live in, he is worrying about the same things that made old hairy frown and snort in his peculiar way:

how to keep out the cold and rain;
how to keep in the warmth;
how to make the place stand up;
how to stop the damp of the earth from rising into the dwelling;
how to let the smoke out;
how to let the light in.

These, and a few more we have invented since, such as noise, are the chief problems of house building, and it is to find an answer to these pressing questions that man has gone out into the country round him in search of suitable materials.

6 A hut of bamboo, mud and grass to ward off sun and rain and keep out evil spirits by night. (West Africa.)

What did he find? That is a large question when you remember how the climates and countries of the world vary from icy cold to uncomfortably hot. For the Eskimo, the most important thing is keeping out the cold. Whereas for the African Negro rain and heat may be the principal worries. In fact the world is so varied and the peoples of the world so unlike in their intelligence and habits, that today you will find every kind of dwelling, from the primitive cave, through tents, mud huts, basket-work cages on poles, to the most complicated sky-scrapers, all suiting somebody's idea of what a dwelling should be. The idea comes first.

7 A house as strong as the storms: even the roof is made of stone slabs. A farmhouse in the north of England.

First you must feel a need for a dwelling: because you are too cold, or too hot, because you want to shelter from danger, because you want to store your food, or because you want all these simple and necessary things and a lot more.

Let us consider one of the great needs first: how to keep out the weather. There has always been the weather to keep out – sun, rain, hail, snow, wind, fog. What has man found to do this job?

He has found leaves and branches, heather, all kinds of grasses, straw and reeds, which he has learnt to plait and weave together and to bind down into a compact mass, tilting it sideways so that the rain can run off on to the ground. He has always used these simple materials, which he has never failed to find near at hand.

In stone countries he has made a roof of thin stones or slate, but he could only do this when the stone split easily, otherwise it would have been too thick and heavy to support. Slate is the stone most easily split, and that is why it has been so much used in England. It was cheap and light, but this thin slate that came from the mountain quarries in Wales was dark blue in colour and very uninteresting to look at. The builders who used it did not like it particularly, but thought only of money. Few people like it today. But there it is, millions of tons of it, ready to be used some day.

Very early in our history, we found how useful mud could be. Playing about with mud is one of our first discoveries. Mix a little water with dust or clay and it becomes squashy and can be shaped with the fingers or a piece of wood or some simple tool. Leave it in the sun and it becomes hard. It also cracks, but if a little straw or fibre is mixed with it although it may crack very slightly, in the main it will hold together, and with skill the cracks can be eliminated. Out of this mud, or for preference, clay and straw, man has been making bricks and tiles for thousands of years. The bricks he used for walls and the tiles, light in weight, and most pleasant in colour, he has used for roofs. What an invention!

When man first found metals and learnt how to separate them from the rock and to melt them, it was for weapons and tools that he used them. As they became more plentiful, he took to using them for building. But metal is heavy, and no one thought of covering a roof with it until most of the problems of roof building had been solved.

The great things about metal as a covering for roofs are, first, that it keeps out the weather absolutely, and next that it lasts nearly for ever. The Romans used to make little tiles or plates of bronze, overlapping them and fitting them neatly together. They used these on their most important buildings. But lead is the metal one thinks of in connection with roofs, and medieval churches and cathedrals are the buildings it was used for. Lead as used in building is bendable. It is made in thin sheets that can be cut with a sharp knife, and nails can be driven through it with ease. This means that it can be done into rolls like cloth, and can be unrolled on to a wooden roof and nailed down; and so long as the joints are carefully made and well beaten down, it will keep out the weather for hundreds of years. But it is extremely heavy, and extremely expensive! The great cathedrals were built with the strongest arches and timbers so as to be able to carry the weight of the lead-covered roof. It was worth it, of course. To keep the rain out of a cathedral was worth a lot of effort.

8 Burnt clay for Mediterranean heat: the ancient Roman tile continuing to fulfil its purpose. (Italy.)

Copper keeps out the weather as well as lead does and is both thin and light. It, too, is expensive and in the past was only used to cover the twiddly things like spires and little domes, and only occasionally on bigger

9 The major building problem of the Middle Ages: how to make a permanent roof for an everlasting building.

domes. It turns a pale green after a time, and is a lovely covering for a roof.

When we speak of metals you must realise that we are concerned only with very important buildings – churches, palaces, and the like. Lesser buildings went on using straw and reeds, split stone, and slate, and tiles. It wasn't until the nineteenth century that metal became cheap enough for general use, and then in a sense it became too cheap.

Steel sheets, pressed for greater strength into a wavy pattern or corrugation, were a nineteenth-century solution of the roof problem, and they have been used in every part of the world. They certainly keep the rain out, but they will not keep the sun out, will not keep the warmth in, will not last more than a few years and look as cheap and ignoble as in fact they are. Corrugated iron is too easy a solution to please us for very long.

So too is asbestos cement, another factory-made material that is cheap, light, weather-resisting, but impermanent and unlovely to look at or to handle.

There is another material called reinforced concrete from which roofs of many shapes and types can be made. We will talk about this material later; for the moment we will say only that it makes a very strong roof, which can be flat, or carved or domed to nearly any size; but it leaks. Tiny little cracks develop and the rain trickles through. Fortunately, after a little searching a proper covering was found for it, asphalt. This comes from lakes in Trinidad, large, burning lakes of asphalt, and also from mines. It is heated in a cauldron, poured over the concrete roof and there becomes solid, though not absolutely rock hard. It will be impervious to rain for years and years. The sun

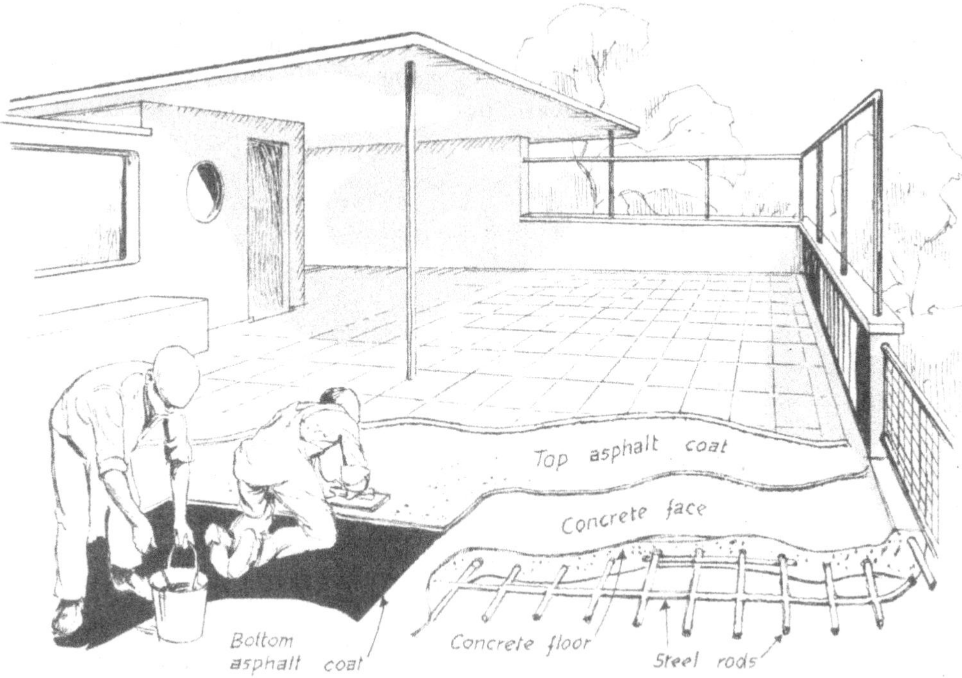

10 The old problem of how to keep out the weather: workmen applying asphalt to the roof of a modern house. The roof is cut away to show the reinforced concrete, asphalt, and top cover of paving.

will melt it slightly on hot summer days, but the rain puddles may lie on it indefinitely, for none will seep through.

Scientists have been busily finding substitutes for natural materials such as wood, wool, cotton, rubber, etc., in the course of which they have produced a whole range of synthetic plastics which are finding their way into architecture as roof lights, panels and finally as complete roofs unlike any that we have dealt with hitherto, and which will provoke changes that we will talk about later.

All these materials are answers to the eternal question of how to keep the weather out of the dwelling, and principally the weather that falls on us from above, in the form of rain and sun and snow. This is not the whole story. You may keep the rain from you by holding up an umbrella, but if you had no clothes on it would not solve the problem at all. A roof is all that is needed to protect a haystack, but man feels the cold that comes at him from all directions: he must make a cold-proof shelter.

So we must think now of the other things besides coverings for the roof: we must think about the whole building and how to make it.

It would be a good thing if we stopped ranging all over the world and through history and settled on one spot by way of example. Four or five hundred years ago in England hundreds of little houses were built by small farmers – we like to think of them as free, sturdy yeoman farmers – which we treasure today because they are beautiful and made of beautiful materials. Illustration 11 shows one of these old cottages, of the very simplest kind. What can it tell us?

First you must imagine that farmer–builder clearing a space for himself amid the forests that covered so much of England in those distant times. He would have had some still simpler dwelling before he decided to build this one, was already cultivating some fields with crude ploughs drawn by oxen, kept a horse or two, stored some food, and had a family to be fed, warmed and cooked for. He was a man with definite wants.

It is doubtful whether he could either read or write, for neither were of great use to him. Furthermore he had the church and the monastery at hand to teach him his duty to God, and his lord to exact his duty to worldly authority. He was unlettered but not unlearned.

This man, with his pressing needs to satisfy, looked about him as man had been looking since the dawn of history for materials with which to keep his family from bad weather and danger, to keep them and his goods safe and secure in the years to come.

He had reached the stage of needing a fire for cooking as well as for warmth, and this is an important factor that took hundreds of years to solve satisfactorily. He could consider himself lucky to find men who baked bricks near enough to his farm to be hauled by his oxen. You may be certain that he thought himself a rich and successful farmer to be able to afford bricks for his fire

11 The basic English house, built of the materials of the earth it stands on.

and chimney, but how rich you may judge when you know that he only used bricks for this part of the house. They were too rare for anything more; and transport was far too difficult. So he built his fireplace and chimney, spanning the wide opening of the fire with a great branch or tree-trunk roughly hewn into shape with an adze, for the saw had not yet been invented.

He would also go into the forest in search of crooked trees or branches. He was after trees that were slightly bowed, like the timbers of a ship, and he soon found what he wanted – six or eight fine pieces about 6 metres long, which, when he had lopped off the branches, he could erect, in pairs, with two ends stuck into the earth, and the other two ends fastened together at the top. They must have looked rather like large chicken wishbones, pointed at the top and curved below. This was his most difficult task. The rest of the timbers were smaller, since their job was, first, to hold the main timbers or principals together, and then to make a sort of large basket pattern on which to fix the walls, and then the roof.

He had now made his main structure. It looked like an upturned boat. For his roof he had been cutting straw into lengths, or perhaps reeds he cut from the marsh near by. These he bound into little bundles and fastened and pegged down, layer after layer, until he had a fine thick coating on each side of his structure, brought up to a neat ridge and cut off in a good even line at the height of his door. He made his door and the line of his thatching eaves low so as to throw off the rain and protect his wall. He was fairly certain that his thatched roof would keep out the rain, but the walls still gave him trouble.

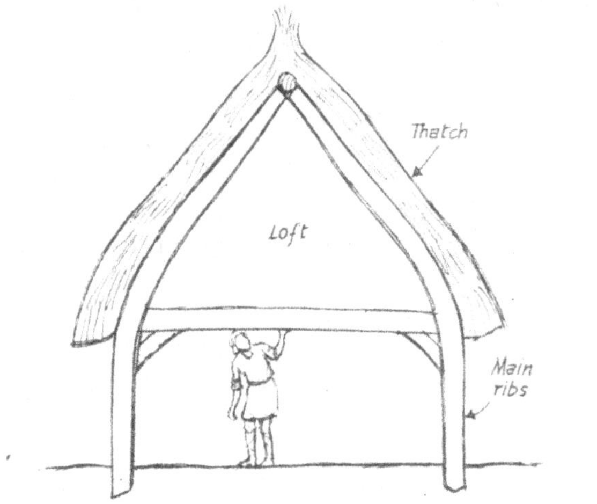

13 The simplest cottage structure. It looks like a wishbone, and has lasted 500 years.

12 The farmer–builder at work on his house of timber, mud, bricks and thatch.

Mud was the best he could do for a wall – mud and sticks. His solution of this problem was to take some pliant pieces of stick which he wove in basket fashion and fixed between the larger timbers to act as a base and a reinforcement to the well-kneaded clayey soil, filled in between the timbers. We call this idea 'wattle and daub'. Not a very good wall, but if well enough guarded by overhanging eaves, fairly lasting and warm.

The door was easy enough, but windows were a great trouble and expense. If the small English farmer of the sixteenth century could afford to buy glass and iron, even the cheapest bull's-eye glass that few people wanted in those days, it was a sign that English farming was in a good state. Actually an iron window with leaded lights was such a possession that it was moved with the owner as one would move a grand piano today.

The house that our farmer–builder showed so proudly to his wife and family, if indeed they did not help to make it, was weather-proof, strong, and lasting. It was nearly all roof, very low-ceilinged, and had the smallest windows, but it was a winter house, built for the worst conditions, not all conditions. As the floor was of beaten clay and the walls of mud it could not be proof against earth damp, but with this exception it fulfilled all the essential needs of a countryman and his family, and continued to do so for hundreds of years: a sufficiently good proof of the farmer's intelligence and skill.

He could sit at his porch and have within view the source of all its materials, the fields of wheat, the forests, the clay of the surrounding earth that made his walls and his bricks – everything but the iron and the glass, those new treasures which in course of time were to transform the art of his building.

What we have described here was the norm of building nearly anywhere in the world before the machine age. It produced building of a variety that arose directly from the varied local circumstances, and these gave it its shape, its texture, and its character.

When the Pilgrim Fathers reached America they carried with them memories of the English farmer's craft but they faced a new set of circumstances, with harder winters to deal with, and these slight differences produced the New England frame house, typically American.

But this little picture of a man at work gives you your first clue to architecture, which is the art of good building. First you have wants, simple or complicated, and to meet these you will look for materials of the right kind. In the sixteenth century you use what you find near at hand. In the twentieth century you use the best and cheapest of all those that you can buy from near and far, and that will be sent to you by road, rail or air. The choice is wider, and the wants more numerous, but the main problems are the same: how to keep out wind and weather, how to keep in warmth.

14 A casement window, one of the earliest luxuries of simple building.

The farmer's house was weakest in the walls because he was using a very old system of walling better done perhaps by many an African tribe. The church he went to would have stone walls, and the new manor house going up in the manorial meadows would have walls of brick, for everywhere his world was looking to newer and better ways of building and was not in the least sentimental about its lovely buildings.

Since then we have invented only one or two newer systems of walling, of which the first is reinforced concrete, which we

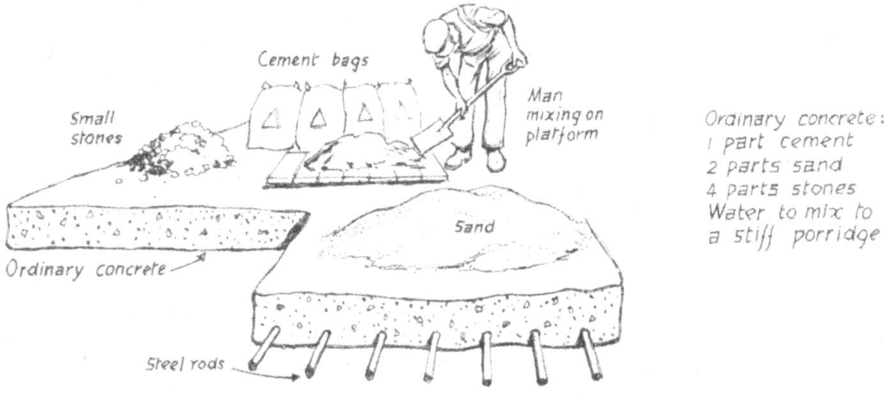

15 How to make concrete the simple way. On the left, ordinary concrete. On the right, concrete strengthened with steel rods.

mentioned earlier. Bricks are made of clay and water mixed together and reinforced with a little straw. Concrete is made of limestone crushed to a fine powder called cement, mixed with a little water, and reinforced by sharp sand and hard pieces of stone.

As the water dries out, the cement hardens as clay does, only more so. Like clay it cracks as it hardens, but the sand and stones act like the straw in bricks so that the cracks never properly develop. Hard though it is, and nearly uncrushable, these cracks are a weakness and concrete is no good for the jobs that timber does so well, such as bridging gaps and taking weights in the middle of a span. It is all right in the mass, but as a post or a beam it is too liable to break or crack under stress. It has no strong grain like timber. It is like a rock-cake.

The Romans used concrete a good deal, even above the great domes of their temples and public baths. Then it fell into disuse as first iron and then steel took its place, until in the nineteenth century a gardener, so the story goes, found that pieces of steel bedded in concrete gave it immense strength, not only against pressure but against bending and cracking. This was an invention of the greatest importance, for it gave us a material of which to make walls, floors, roofs, the complete structure, in fact. Reinforced concrete is one of the outstanding building systems of our time.

Glass is another. The sixteenth-century farmer would barely connect the modern glass window with the funny little casement he got with such effort.

The other problem unsolved or unthought of by the farmer was that of the dampness from the earth. In rainy and swampy places such as Malaya the custom is to build houses on poles driven into the swamp – a neat solution to a difficult problem. In England, because we have to deal with dampness rather than wet, we have been apt to overlook it in the past, though dampness is nearly as dangerous to health as wetness. To overcome the danger we now lay a raft of concrete over the site of the building, and if it is very damp we cover this with a layer of asphalt or some other damp-proof material, and some more concrete to make certain that no water rises through. Then we lay a strip of waterproof material, or asphalt or lead, or a layer of slates low down in each wall that goes into the ground, and when this is done the house is sure to be dry.

What other problems are there in the building of a house? What other needs are there to be met? Light must be let in. Men

16 Damp entering primitive building through walls and floor.

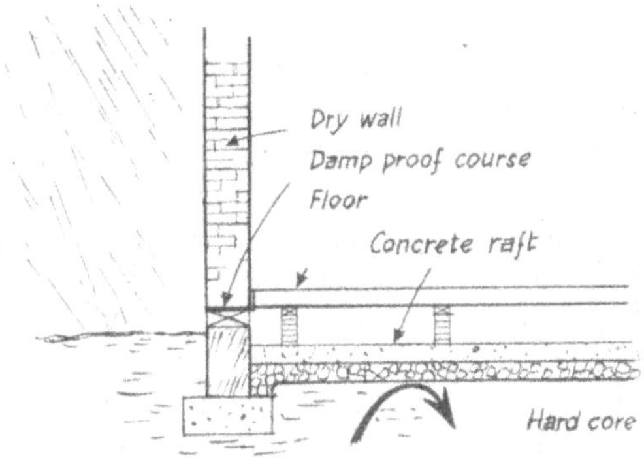

17 Damp defeated by concrete foundations and rafts and a damp-proof course acting as a barrier.

18 Cooking at its most primitive: the open fire of the early Middle Ages.

first did this simply by leaving holes, which were covered by shutters in bad weather and open in good; or were covered by skin, and finally by glass.

How big these holes or windows are to be depends on a number of things such as how peaceful life is outside the house, how large glass sheets can be made and how cheaply. It depends on how warm you can keep the inside of the house, because big windows let light in but if not facing the sun will let heat out. Finally, it depends on the materials of which the house is built, for brick and stone have limitations that do not trouble steel, concrete or glass.

Then there is the problem of warmth. The first obvious answer is to light a fire and risk the consequences, and for hundreds of years this was the only answer. The inside used to get filled with smoke when the wind blew from the wrong quarter, and great streamers of soot hung from the rafters. But as these went with a rough and smelly life, with dirt and fleas in abundance, it was only one problem among many.

It got solved in time: the result was the fireplace and chimney. You will remember that the farmer–builder's chimney was his chief work. He was right up to the minute in having a fireplace and chimney.

The open fireplace spelt draughts, from the doors and windows, and up the chimney; draughts in the warmest place in the room! Our ancestors built settles round the fire, and had great armchairs, and screens, but they could never cure draught so long as the fireplace remained open.

Now, to have heat where it is wanted and without draughts is a problem we have solved in a number of ways. We send it round the house in hot water pipes. We send it round in electric wires to which are connected radiators and fires of various kinds. We send it round in ducts under the floor nearly exactly as the Romans did, or

19 When kitchens became separated from living-rooms the fireplace became the formal centre of the room and was ornamented accordingly.

20 The centre of life in the farmhouse: cooking, heating and social life in one. We are returning to this system with our modern living-room–kitchen.

we air-condition it. There will be more about this later.

Then there is the question of cooking. The simple solution is to cook and eat round the same fire. There is nothing as good as camp-fire cooking – for a short time. The farmhouse system of eating near the fire – the farmhouse kitchen meal – is as good a way of eating as there is, economical of time and effort and friendly into the bargain.

We have learnt to separate eating from cooking, to have two rooms, two chimneys, two of everything, where once one was enough. We have complicated life to this extent, but whether we have lost or gained is hard to say. It is all a matter of what you want. We learnt to separate different kinds of work as we came to live in towns, but as long as we build houses, we must cook – by fire, gas or electricity, and cook and eat in one room if we are poor, and two if we are not.

The easiest solution to the washing problem is not to. Millions of people wash seldom if ever. Some oil themselves, and others only wash in summer. In early days it was a cold wash or nothing. Those were the days of summer washing.

Then there was the ceremonial wash in a tub before the fire with big black kettles simmering on the hearth. Thousands of London houses, built in the last century, had no bathrooms. For that was the age of the tin bath set out in the bedroom with the hot water can brought up by the maid. It was the age of the tin bath for the few and no wash for the many.

The modern bath appeared only when we had learnt how to send hot water through pipes from a boiler, and had built drains to take the water away. Nowadays we bring cold water to houses and heat it, but in some other countries man has had the idea of bringing hot water, as well as cold, to the house. If this can be managed cheaply, it is a great advantage. There are two other main problems which we have still to solve better than we do: disposing of our rubbish and sewage.

21 This is how the Victorian gentleman took his bath, with servants to wait upon him.

The modern water closet, sometimes miscalled lavatory, is really a very simple and satisfactory piece of machinery. (A lavatory is really a place where you wash, and the word comes from the Latin verb *lavare*, meaning to wash.) The water closet is an invention that has made life pleasanter. It makes it possible for human excrement to be taken away by a system of pipes to a place where it is treated by chemicals and made harmless or useful. The water closet, by keeping some water in what is called the 'trap', prevents foul air and smells from coming into the house. If you had lived about a hundred years ago, you would not have had this and life would have been more smelly and less pleasant.

There is the larger problem of waste which we have failed to solve. In medieval times you threw it out into the street, or dumped it outside the town walls, and fouled the rivers, and brought on plague. Even so there were not enough people about to do real damage, and it was not until we began to crowd people into the industrial and urban slums that we contaminated our water supply on a large scale and cholera spread through cities.

But now in this age of so-called plenty the problem comes to us from several sides, for we are so numerous and live so largely in cities, closely packed together and cut off from the sources of our food supply.

Then our food and goods come to us extravagantly packed in cans and containers, bulky and largely indestructible. The food waste that should go back on the land, as it does in China, is mixed up with the rest. When all this is collected it must be dumped, or burnt and made harmless or useful, at a cost in wages and equipment that is becoming a typical nightmare of city government and part of the world problem of pollution, which is going to be more and more the concern of us all. If you could see what an elaborate and costly kind of factory a waste disposal plant is you would see what we mean.

It all flows from the realisation of how removed we are from the simple building needs of the yeoman farmer, for when people gather into cities by the thousand and the million their needs cannot be simply satisfied.

Instead of a house we must talk of housing and instead of asking each person what he or she wants, we – and that means whoever builds the houses, whether public authority or private contractor or financier – must assume what people want and hope it suits them.

This is not as crude as it sounds. A great deal of research and experiment goes on all the time as one of the major responsibilities of architects and those who work with them, and as a result housing standards improve and styles change. In England alone we have built over thirty new towns, each one a sort of experiment, and the search continues.

We have dealt almost entirely with the house and housing but the problem of shelter has been enormously changed and enlarged by the conditions of modern life.

Not that Westminster Abbey was a small building, or the great roof of St Stephen's Hall a small span. Far from it. Yet we could today with comparative ease throw a perspex and aluminium dome over either of them, and for the Olympic Games we create enormous interior spaces in reinforced concrete and glass, and auditoria holding many thousands of people.

There are in fact few limits to what we can now construct by way of shelter. One ingenious engineer has suggested that we build a whole town under one great dome and so live independent of all weathers, but this is an idea that we regard with some suspicion, still believing that natural weather has its solid benefits as well as its discomforts. Nevertheless we now have very large shopping and cultural centres under one roof with their own artificial climates of conditioned air. We can throw bridges miles long over great rivers under which tall ships pass. It must be admitted that though we have by no means solved the problem of shelter at the domestic level, at other levels we have achieved wonders.

22 A modern shopping centre sheltered from the sun and rain. Technology serving social needs. (Vällingby, Sweden.)

3
Living, Working and Moving

The Arrangement of Space

In the last chapter we have been trying to discover why human beings in general need buildings, what they have invented and what they have done to meet this need in the world so far.

You know now that building and architecture are concerned with most pressing and important matters, and that these matters are to be attended to before everything else. You may also have some suspicion that in spite of everything science has done for us, these primary matters have not always been settled to everybody's satisfaction. Whether they are dealt with efficiently or not depends on many people, on you when you are old enough to take a hand, on the architects, the builders, the workmen, the manufacturers, the officials, and on many more who have smaller parts to play. No longer is a house built by the man who will afterwards live in it, for life has changed since our farmer–builder bent over his work on the roof-tree of his own home; we have learnt to divide the labour of building among many brains and hands, and to see it whole we must know what each of these part-workers does, and through what processes the work of creation now moves.

The first thing an architect or anyone who sets out to build has to do, is to imagine the activities that are to be sheltered, housed, or protected by the building. Simple activities, such as storing a quantity of hay, do not require much imagining, but they require some, because the hay must be taken in and taken out, it might catch fire, and it might not. When you are setting out to build a hay barn, you must know these things, and you must be able to imagine what happens in and about a hay barn, so as to be able to provide everything necessary, and have the right tools and enough materials on the spot when the work starts. If you were doing it yourself it would matter less if you forgot something, because you could kick yourself, quietly slip away for the missing stuff, and then make up for being a fool by working harder. But when someone else does the work, or several people do it, it is well to be able to think of everything in advance.

When it comes to a family house the problem is already quite complicated, more so than many an engineering or scientific problem, and for the simple reason that people are involved in every part of it.

A house looks a settled enough affair and

of course we get used to the house we live in. Whatever sort of house it is, we furnish and decorate it in our own way; things have their fixed and well-understood positions; and if we have grown up in it, we know its dark corners and its peculiar noises and smells, and it has, so to speak, become a part of us.

But all houses have to be designed and built to start with, and already you know how much houses have changed over the centuries from 'wattle and daub' shelters to the latest 'ranch type, split level' or whatever jargon describes the speculators' glowing offer to the newly married couple.

Whatever the house is it grows out of and tries to cater for the manifold activities of a family.

Now one thing we all do in a fairly orderly and standard way is to sleep. We spend a lot of our lives sleeping, so that in most two-storeyed houses, and these are the great majority of houses, the first floor consists of bedrooms, a bathroom and a staircase and passage to reach them.

By the same token the ground floor consists of living-rooms, a way into the house and a way upstairs. So there are two main elements, the living and sleeping spaces, and the means of getting to and from them, which are the communication spaces.

In the past century vast areas of London were built on a very simple plan that differed little as between smaller and larger terrace houses. It has a hall and staircase, a parlour in front, a dining-room at the rear, a kitchen in the basement, and bedrooms on all other floors. There were no bathrooms or w.c.s to start with, and these houses, down to a surprisingly low social level, depended on servants to do the fetching and carrying so that the owners could live in genteel respectability.

A great deal has happened since then to change the character and the mechanics of a normal house. First came water in pipes from distant reservoirs into each house; and then came gas to light and heat it and to replace the old cast-iron range in the basement kitchen. But by far the most important was what went out, for the w.c. and its pipes, drains, sewers and disposal plants must have changed people's lives more than anything else.

What came later in the form of electricity, telephone, central heating of various kinds, air-conditioning, radio and television, cookers, refrigerators, dishwashers and so on, were luxuries compared with the drainage.

And so we have to think of a lot of new communication systems, for that is what they are, flowing along pipes and wires to wherever we want them or they should be.

23 Our legacy of simple urban terrace houses of the eighteenth and nineteenth century. Adaptable and versatile, they have served us well.

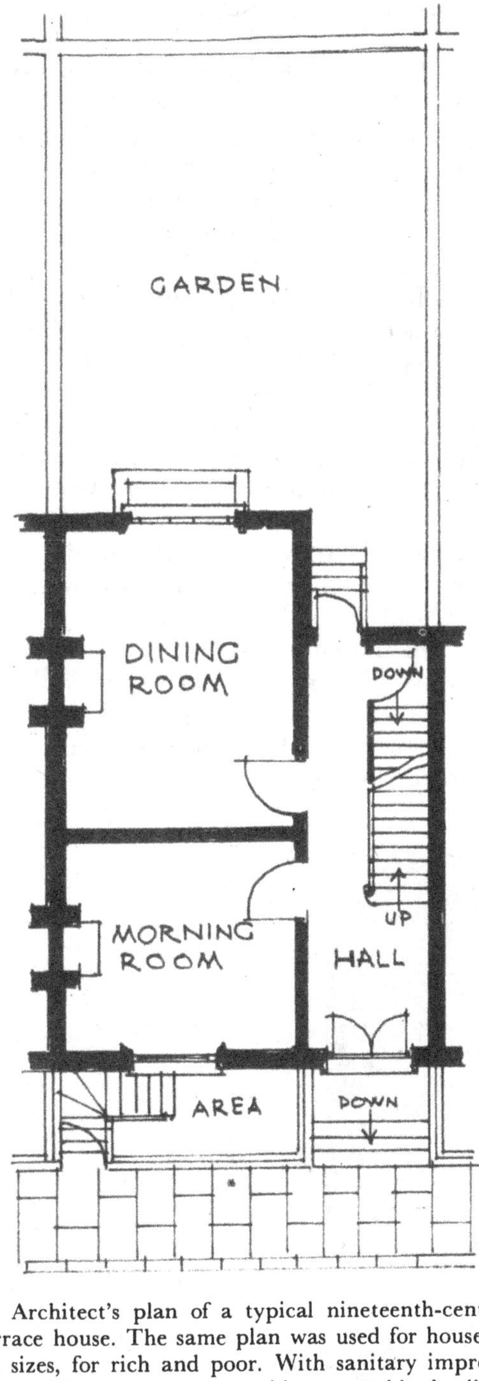

24 Architect's plan of a typical nineteenth-century terrace house. The same plan was used for houses of all sizes, for rich and poor. With sanitary improvements they continue to provide acceptable dwellings in an urban setting.

They are expensive, and cost being a hard master, we must reduce piping and drainage to the minimum, leading us therefore to place bathrooms over, or nearly over, kitchens, with the vertical pipes grouped together or shared. Another factor, which is much neglected in both England and America, is aspect. Our north and north-east faces are vulnerable to cold and cold wind; our south and south-west get the sun and rain, but not so much cold. Larders used always to be placed on the north and north-east, and living-rooms of any kind should enjoy the sun.

But time has brought many changes. We keep food in refrigerators, though it costs more, and instead of heating each room with a fire we heat the whole house with hot water pipes, or hot or conditioned air, and are more flexible and can be much more open with our living spaces. Indeed our kitchen apparatus is so clean and bright – the fumes taken off by electric fans – that it can become part of our living area; can be in fact a part of the living-room itself. Being only ourselves with no servant to banish to the kitchen we revert to something approaching the sociable farmhouse living-room which was the centre of family life.

A house then, is a series of enclosed air spaces, each shaped and fitted for a definite activity, most of them living spaces with a few passage or circulation spaces. The problem for the architect is how much space can be allowed for the whole house and how much of it for each separate activity in it. This is the eternal problem of space versus cost.

Many people imagine that architects are only concerned with appearances and decoration. A very few are. But for most of them cost is a prime consideration and in order not to start on designs that will cost too much, an architect relies on records of what similar buildings have cost in the recent past, usually expressed at so many pounds for each square metre of floor area.

These ruling costs are constantly being brought up to date and are published in magazines. They are very important because the great majority of dwellings are paid for by government money, and the amount is limited. There is what is called a 'ceiling' of cost which must not be exceeded. If the ceiling cost of a three-bedroom dwelling is £8,000, and the cost of building is £80 per square metre, then the architect knows from the beginning that the house cannot be larger than 100 square metres spread over everything, one floor of a flat or two floors of a maisonette. And that is that.

So an architect starting on the design, let us say, of a single unit in a large group of buildings – and we are taking one particular maisonette, No. 18 Maran Way in the new town of Thamesmead near Woolwich on the lower Thames – is not free to do just as he likes. He is already working within a wider idea, he is bound by the general conception of the whole scheme as a large piece of environment, and he is bound by a money ceiling.

But there are benefits built into this situation. Thamesmead is a very big adventure in idealism. It is a town in which the pedestrian comes first and the motor-car second. But more than this, the planners set out to improve the quality of life for Londoners.

We will talk about its planning later in the book. It is enough to say here that the long terrace in which No. 18 is situated is connected by safe footways to anywhere in the town – to school, to the shops, to the lake, to the bus, and out of the town into the preserved woodlands in the background. How unusual to have these vital questions settled before the dwelling is designed!

The first condition laid down is that all outside walls must be at least 5.340 metres apart. On the entrance side of No. 18 is a wide walkway; on the other side, looking west, a parkway. It is a large maisonette for a family of five. The architect has used reinforced concrete as the main material,

25 Model of Thamesmead. An imaginative and humane city extension to London, which separates traffic from people and brings the great river back into daily living.

26 No. 18 Maran Way, a large maisonette overlooking the parkway and forming part of a new style terrace.

which has enabled him to take the large bedroom area over the walkway or access deck, which is now a covered one, leaving a really wide balcony overlooking the open space on the other side of the house.

Now comes the struggle for space – daylit space for bedrooms and living-rooms; unlit or electrically lit space for cupboards and bathrooms. Bathrooms had once to be on an outside wall, lit and ventilated naturally, and this is always to be preferred. An internal bathroom is possible only because we can trust an electric fan to keep working nearly indefinitely, though it can be turned on and off by a switch.

There is another point relating to heating. The open fire was once the only means of heating, whether it was a coal or a gas fire. We can now push heat around in pipes and radiators, or we can push air around in ducts, and both these systems heat the whole dwelling, not just parts of it. This is a great freedom, but we lose the family fireside as the centre of life, and tend to put the television set in its place.

Knowing these things before starting, the architect was able to achieve four good daylit rooms on the bedroom floor, and to put into the darker interior the bathroom, the essential storage cupboards, the stairs and the very important 'service core': the machine room of the dwelling, you might call it, from which come hot water, hot air and other pipes.

What a marvellous little jigsaw of planning it is, this cluster of cupboards and pipes that still leaves plenty of space for the stairs and doors opening on to lovely rooms flooded with light, the largest for the parents, the next for the children, the third for the teenager, and the fourth for some privacy for whoever needs it most; a really flexible arrangement that can last a growing family for years.

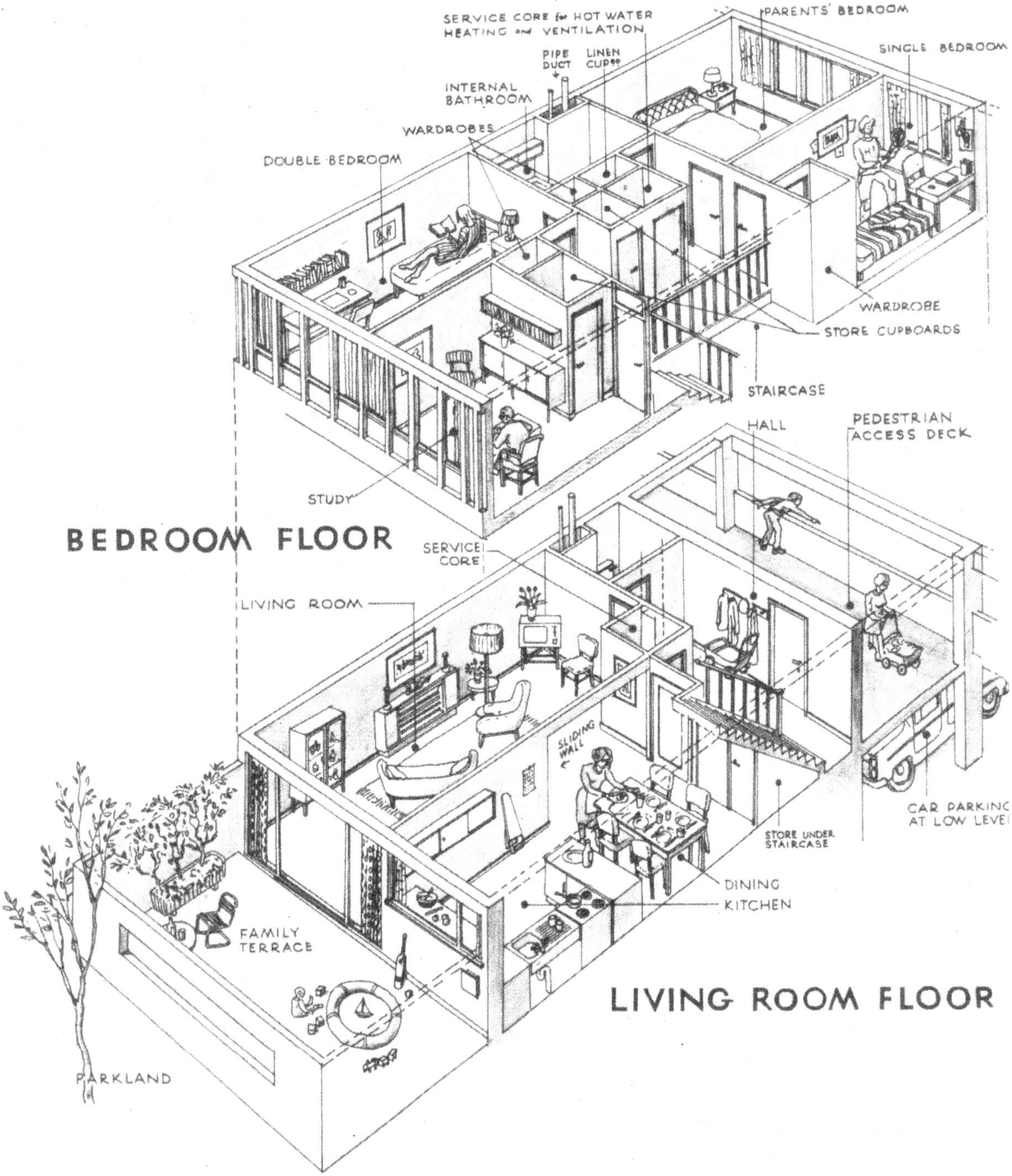

27 The activities and the mechanics of No. 18 Maran Way exposed to show how all elements interlock to provide a workable and livable home.

On the floor below, however, everything is spacious. You will notice that the 'service core' comes from above and that the essentials of the ground floor cloakroom are under the bathroom. The stairs pop up out of the hall in the corner, and the hall is big enough to take a pram.

The living-room is a good size. It joins the balcony, with its flowers or its toys, to become an even bigger space; and in addition, it can be extended by means of a wide sliding door into the dining space and the kitchen itself. The family can eat in the kitchen, or enjoy the larger space, all of it heated equally by the warm air circulating from the 'service core'.

Before leaving No. 18 let us remember the traditional house of the past, with its parlour, its living-room so often thrust into the background, and its kitchen thrust out into the garden. This was in many ways a historical relic and by comparison No. 18 is freedom and light.

Now we must walk out of the house in search of a bigger building, because we do not spend all of our time at home. Fathers and mothers go out to work in factories and offices, they go out shopping, and boys and girls go out to school. So we will go out along the walkway above the traffic and out of harm's way. There below us is a primary school with its playgrounds and trees growing up around them almost as though it was in the country. It is called Southlake Primary School, because it stands near the South Lake.

Now a school is a largish problem for an architect. Not five people to makes spaces for, but five hundred perhaps. It is the same sort of problem on a larger scale. Instead of bedrooms, kitchen and so on, it is classrooms, hall, gymnasium, science room, art room and the like, plus a dining-room and kitchen, the inevitable corridors and staircases and lavatories. All this has to be

28 The school from its playground. Formal architecture combined with flowers and greenery.

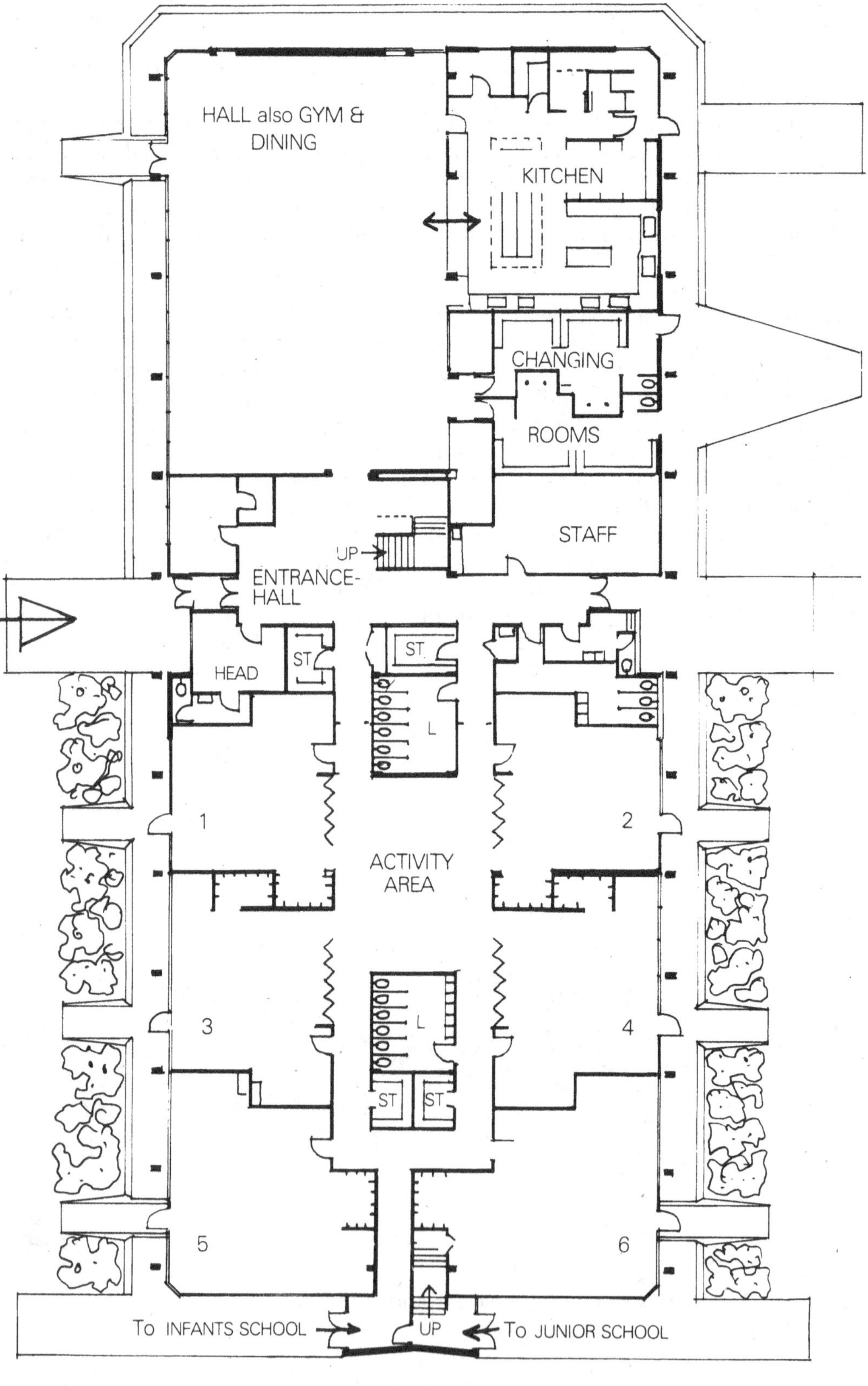

29a Southlake Primary School: ground floor plan.

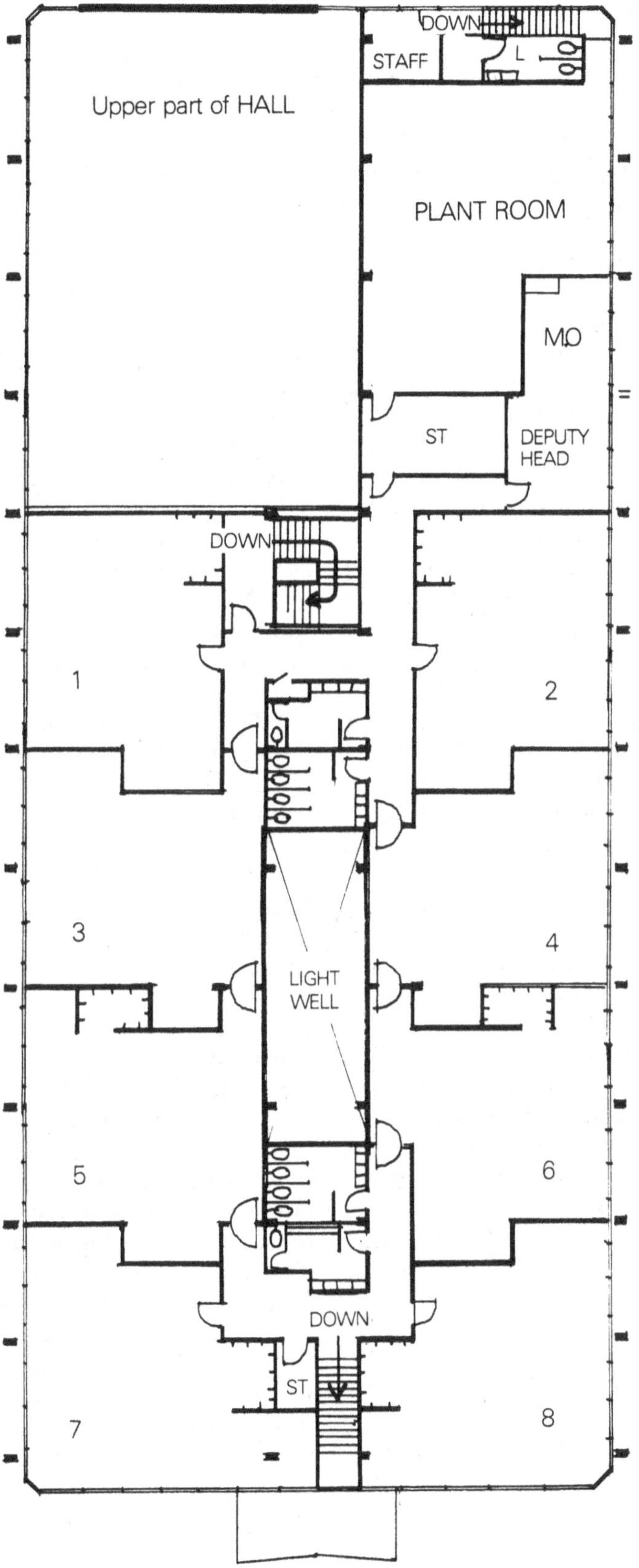

29b Southlake Primary School: first floor plan.

brought together under one roof at a cost that is very carefully inquired into by the authorities, and in such a way that it works harmoniously and provides a background for the years of a school child's life that will be remembered.

Just as the architect who designed No. 18 Maran Way was not free to do what he liked but had to fit himself into the general scheme of Thamesmead and keep within limits of cost already laid down, so the architect of Southlake Primary School had to fit into the scheme and keep to a budget.

But the scheme of Thamesmead is a generous one. This primary school is not wedged between two streets as it might once have been. It sits within a large area of playing fields in which the actual playgrounds, which would once have been the only open spaces, are mere incidents in the layout.

Then at the east end there is the lake, that is joined to other waterways of the new town. On all sides are lawns, trees and plants, and from the school entrance level ramps ascend taking children over the motor traffic safely home. What a preparation for a mere primary school, you might say. But for the new towns a school is a most precious object, in itself and as a part of the community.

Even so this school's budget was limited and it was planned as carefully as a dwelling where every penny counts. It is in the form of a long two-storey box supported by thirteen rows of rather heavy columns carrying a floor and a roof slab with holes left in them along the central line to bring light and air to a rather wide floor. In one corner the space goes through two floors to make a grand and airy assembly hall.

This sounds too simple. It sounds as though the architect was taking the easiest course. But his decision to keep the envelope of the building simple could have been influenced by the simple lines of the surrounding townscape as well as by the need for economy. Simple things well done are better than any amount of showing-off.

It is a rather severe and uncompromising building, but in twenty years' time, when it stands bowered in trees and flowers, these lines will be grand rather than oppressive.

Inside it is positively ingenious: it fits in six infant classes on the ground floor and eight junior classes on the first floor, with their cloakrooms and lavatories and separate ways up. The juniors on the first floor are segregated as they attend to their lessons, the infants rather more free to move around, as they are not ready yet for formal learning. Then at one end, separated from the classrooms, are the staff and the head master and the much used hall which functions as assembly area, dining-room and gymnasium, with a background of kitchens and changing rooms and the plant to keep it all going. All parts are light and airy despite the heavy columns on the outside, and very little space is wasted on circulation. Nor could you find a more economical placing of the lavatories, one above the other along the centre line of the plan, so that, as in No. 18 Maran Way where the bathrooms and heating unit are in the centre of the plan, the outer walls are entirely free to let in light from every side but the north.

Let us not forget the details that keep the architect to his drawing board for so long before work can start. They will not show much in this building because of its simplified organisation, but they are there – the boilers, the heating and hot water pipes, the waste and the soil pipes on their way through the building to the sewers, and the sewerage scheme for treating the waste before it is released to our old polluted river, which we will clean as never before. There are also the electrical wires to lights and power points, and lastly the highly equipped kitchen which generations of cooks, engineers, committees, dieticians and, of course, architects, have brought to a marvel of perfection for its prime purpose – to cook and serve appetising food quickly to a hungry hoard without wasting time or money.

Through all this you will have noticed how important space is: large space for the assembly hall, small space for the lavatory; tiny little spaces for pipes to creep along or pop up through; but space organised, first on plan, then in three dimensions, and finally space harmonised and unified into a single conception, a dwelling, a primary school, an office building, an opera house, a parliament building, whatever human activity we seek to cater for and enclose from wind and weather.

A dwelling and a school. What else? Towns and countryside are made up of all sorts of buildings, but there are more homes than anything else, houses, flats, hotels, hostels; places where people live. A town is like a big house in a way. In a house you have the work place (kitchen etc.), the living space (living-rooms, bedrooms, etc.) and the movement space (passages and stairs). In a town you have the work space for factories, power stations, goods yards, store houses and offices, big shops and markets; the living space for houses, hotels, hostels etc. (this is like the sleeping space in a house), and the recreation space (part of the living space) for parks, gardens, school sports fields, allotments and so on; and of course the movement space for paths, roads, railways, tubes, airports and docks.

In a town, as in a house or a school, the problem is to find the right amount of space for everything so that life can be lived without friction, happily and fully. This is in part the quite practical problem of how to construct railways, roads and sewers, and put up great buildings; and how to pay for these things, to run them when they are built, to maintain them, to collect the fares and the dues, and to administer the whole complicated affair.

But you may look round your towns and say that if this is the work of practical men, then it is high time someone else was given a chance. Don't come to this conclusion too hastily or just because we have suggested it, because the job of doing these things, or rather the job of getting them all done so as to produce a good-looking town, each part helping the whole, is far from easy.

The world is full of individuals wanting individual things: to build a house here, to lay out a factory there, to use this piece of land in a particular way, to fulfil schemes and dreams in their own individual ways. One scheme falls foul of another, and there is quarrelling and bargaining, as there would be no doubt if your school found itself next to a chemical factory and both of you wanted to start building at once. You can see how necessary it is to have some sort of umpire to decide which party has the right to start building. It was the law that decided these things in the past, but though the law may decide between the rights of one man and another, it has never claimed a knowledge of how to plan towns. Therefore we have all agreed that if there is any doubt as to where to lay out roads, and which spaces to keep open and which to build on, it is the town itself that should decide; and by the town we mean those people elected every year to look after the town, the Council or the Corporation, and their permanent officials, among whom we now have a Town Planning Officer, or an architect.

You may wonder why we should have left this job of planning until all our towns were built. What can we possibly do now? Is it not too late?

It sounds a topsyturvy arrangement, we agree. Actually four-fifths of English people live in towns already built; 35 millions out of the 45 millions of us live in built-up towns. But luckily for us towns are much less fixed and permanent than houses. They are always wearing out in different parts, and being rebuilt. Often people who come back to their towns after a long absence look round in a surprised and puzzled way at what has happened in the meantime.

Most of the English towns were built in a hurry; not the really old ones, but the industrial towns and very many of the large cities. No one sat down to work out the living space and work space. No one wondered how much recreation space or movement space would be needed; and of course there was no time for the towns to grow slowly and gracefully. It happened in a hurry, with people tumbling over each other to sink mines, and build factories, shops, offices and houses, houses and houses. Things done hurriedly are done badly, as you know well if you ever try to fasten your shoe-laces with

30 A battleground of interests in which nobody wins.

the last bell ringing. The English towns were built badly by a host of individuals who got in each other's way. And now, more slowly, we are trying to do the job again on a better plan, one in which we get together and agree to give up certain of our old individual rights so that the general spaces of the town may be laid out in a way that enables us all to move about it easily, work happily, find parks and open spaces near at hand, and be in touch with nature whenever we feel like it and without the effort and expense of travelling in buses, trains or tubes.

Although four-fifths of us live in the towns, and although England is one of the more crowded countries of the world, there is a lot of space left over. 'Space left over from the towns' is how we townspeople are apt to regard the country, showing how little we know about farming and market gardening, and how lightly we treat the precious earth from which we get our food, building over it as though it were unlimited, without thought of economy or of the fresh food that year after year it could produce for us.

Now the country is a space, a limited space, and there is another and a better way of using it. First there are work spaces – all the land that can be used without wasted effort to produce food for us. It gives us cereals and vegetables; food for cattle, sheep, horses, hens, ducks, geese and turkeys. It gives us materials in growing timber, in mines and quarries, all manner of richness in return for our work, and for what we put back into the earth. But in so far as we are an industrial nation and make many of our own and other people's necessities in factories, we must set aside a fair amount of space for this purpose, and for the towns that gather round the factories; though it would be silly to waste good farmland or horticultural land on this if we could possibly avoid it, because it takes up to a hundred years to bring land into 'good heart' as the farmers call it, and a hundred years is a long, long time. Therefore, as in the case of the

31 The varied spaces of the countryside, devoted primarily to agriculture but offering release and refreshment for the townsman. Milton Abbas from the air.

32 Gatwick Airport. Compare with illustration 30 to realise how air, road and railway are brought together in a compact plan. But there is still a great toll of farmland, and much noise for miles around.

town, we must get together, and this time it is the County Council, or perhaps the Regional Council, whom we shall ask to settle all questions of how the country space is to be divided and how much is to be left for the use of the townspeople.

When all the useful land is used there is still land that is not much use as work space. There are the great regions of mountain or moor, rocky, devoid of rich soil, too high for heavy trees, the haunts of sheep and curlews. There are rolling downs of fine short grass, useful only as sheep runs. There are the seashores, strewn with rocks or fringed by low dunes, or by mournful mud flats, and marshes where sea-lavender grows. These are the spaces to which townspeople go to refresh themselves, to regain health, strength and happiness. Here should be the country schools to which every town boy and girl should go for some part of every year, the hostels for hikers, the sanatoria for the sick. These are quite properly the recreational spaces, to which, though farming continues, the townspeople have a right of possession and use. England is so varied a country, such a lovely jumble of plains and hills, that no town or city is without its recreational space near at hand. Look for yourself at the map and see whether this is not so.

What other spaces are to be considered? Movement spaces? Yes, the thin lines of pathway, roadway, railway and canal, that spread in an unequally woven network over the country. They do not use a great deal of land, but they cut across it, dividing one part from another, and setting the general public need for movement against more particular and local private needs. Who shall determine the course of the national highways, the railways and canals, if not the State itself, with Parliament for ever on the watch for us, and we ourselves representing public opinion.

We must insert a few words here concerning the unlooked-for effects of the motorcar and the aeroplane, which in the use and possession of vast numbers of relatively rich populations need enormous quantities of land in and over the country, and in and over the towns. This is a problem we are unable to solve to our satisfaction, and the right of the State to make decisions about it has been severely challenged by strong bodies of objecting citizens. It is a problem we shall discuss at the end of the book when we think together of the future.

Then what about those other silent movements? Electrical power carried from the generator stations through the overhead wires of the grid. Water brought to the cities in pipes from the mountain reservoirs, or up deep wells from far below the ground. Will it again be the State that controls the course of these movements?

We have described four types of space – house space, which is a personal and family matter; town space, which is a Council and Corporation matter and a citizen's concern; country space, which is a County or Regional matter; and national power and movements, which are dealt with by the State. There is one more thing we want to say about space: it is relative, by which we mean that it is always to be thought of as being related to human uses, just as unconsciously we measure it with our eyes in terms of our own height or our own movements.

Architects grow familiar with the relationship of spaces to humans and their movements. They know that a dining table should be about 760 mm from the floor, that a bath varies between 1,520 mm and 1,830 mm in length, and between 660 mm and 710 mm in width; that in a busy restaurant you must allow about 1 square metre per person, including passages between tables; that cinema seats should be at least 508 mm wide; that ceilings should not be much lower than 2,440 mm to allow plenty of air for everybody; and that stairs, if they are to be easy to walk up and down, should not be more than 178 mm in the rise or less than 254 mm in the tread. We have only mentioned a few of the relationships, but you will find some more set out for you separately.

It may occur to you that in some places, such as churches, theatres, concert halls, palaces and art galleries, there is a lot of space that is either wasted or not used for anything very obvious. If 2,440 mm is all the height needed in a house where you spend so much time, why make the rooms in palaces or art galleries so very high? There are three reasons we can think of. The first is purely practical: where a number of people are crowded together for any length of time, they need more air to breathe than can be got with a low ceiling; but as we are well able to create forced currents of fresh air with mechanical fans, this is not a reason that operates very strongly, and people aboard Atlantic liners pass their time very happily in large rooms seldom more than 2,290 mm high. The second reason, which applies to kings' palaces, law courts, etc., is that if these spaces are very big you are made to feel small and at the same time you cannot help thinking how great must be the person or the persons, or how powerful must be the law, that so great a space was created for. The other reason, which probably applies to art galleries and similar places, is that after passing much time in small places, shut in by close walls and low ceilings, it does us good to come into big spaces. Next time you are taken to the theatre, to a great cathedral or a fine art gallery, see if you do not have a real feeling of enjoyment when you come through a doorway into the big space. It is as though you were to take deep breaths as you would do on a mountain or by the wide sea. This is what we do when we purposely exaggerate the relationship of space to our own bodies and movements. We remind ourselves of the mountains, the seas and the wide open spaces.

4
How Buildings are Made

Once materials fit for buildings have been found, the next problem is how best to use them. Some materials, such as stone, are nearly ready for use as we find them, and need only to be fitted carefully, one above the other, to make a wall. But if it needs skill to build a dry stone wall, how much more does it need thought, ingenuity and skill to make good use of the other materials we find – to shape them, joint and fix them so that they perform the tasks of protecting us from the weather, keeping the warmth in, letting sun and light in, heating us, giving us water, and so on. Or in architectural terms, we must be able to use them for building walls, floors, roofs, fireplaces and chimneys, for heating, plumbing, stairs, lifts, windows, cupboards, etc., etc.

How is it done, this transformation of raw materials into buildings? In the first case, it is done with a man's brain, his hands and his tools. A man can work wonders unaided. Give him an axe, a spade, a saw, a plane, a hammer and nails, a screwdriver and screws, and he will build a house of sorts that may be lived in. He will sink a well, and dig a ditch, and so live cleanly in his house.

Let him make a forge and he will do more with his hammer, tongs and anvil; he will produce useful and beautiful things.

What he builds will be lowly and humble, dwellings of a kind that delight you wherever you may find them. They will be as simple, as natural, and as beautiful as the nests of birds.

There are limits to what one man can build, yet these limits are infinitely extended by multiplying the number of men engaged on the work and adding some very simple tackle such as scaffold poles, ropes, a jib and pulley, a winding machine. With such means at their disposal the Romans built the mightiest works. Michelangelo had little more for the building of St Peter's with its great dome, and the great cathedrals of England were built in the same way. Men's hands were the chief and best instruments of

33 A log hut: what a man can build with his own hands in primitive conditions.

building and it is men's hands that throughout history of building to the nineteenth century have contributed most to the work.

Building materials were made to be manhandled, especially the brick, the handiest and most useful unit of building ever invented. It was used by the Pharaohs in Egypt, who no doubt borrowed it from someone else, and handed it on to the Greeks, the Romans, the Goths and the English.

We told you how it was made of clay baked in the sun, or burnt in a kiln as we make it now. A brick is made of a size and weight that a man can hold in his left hand. You would find it heavy, but a bricklayer can toss it in the air and hold it while he strikes off a piece with his steel trowel to make it fit somewhere, or while he butters it with a nice dollop of mortar.

When bricks were made entirely by hand they used to be all shapes and sizes. In England it was Sir Christopher Wren who most helped to get bricks made to the same size so that when setting out to build a brick wall, one might know in advance how many bricks to use and not waste time and mortar in filling unequal gaps. Much later a brick size was agreed for the whole country, and this led not only to neat and accurate bricklaying but also to cheap bricks.

A brick wall has three important things to do: hold up the roof that keeps the rain out and the sun off, keep out the rain and winds, and keep in the warmth. Therefore it must be strong, uncrushable and unbendable, solid and free from cracks or holes, and reasonably thick. If you were to lay single bricks straight across the thickness of a wall, the rain would run along the joints, straight into the room, and each brick would simply be lying there without helping the next brick to sit firmly. The great secret of good bricklaying is to bond the bricks, one under, one over, and to bed them in a mortar made of a little cement, some good sharp, well-washed sand and some water, all mixed together, very carefully, and put on fresh when it is like a nice runny porridge.

Starting off on a concrete foundation nearly twice the width of his wall, the bricklayer first stretches a piece of string along the line set out by the architect's drawing kept by the foreman, and lays his first row of bricks. As his wall rises, so he moves up his string. Let us suppose his wall is 215 mm thick with four courses, that is four layers of brick to every 300 mm of height.

When the wall reaches the height of his chest, it is too high for him to work. This is the moment to build the first scaffold of wooden poles or steel tubes, upright from the ground and horizontally from holes he leaves in the wall for the purpose ('putlog holes'), with planks laid across for a working platform, a ladder up to it, and when the next scaffold is reached, a jib and pulley to haul up the mortar, and a bucket of water to soak the bricks in before buttering them with mortar. Each bricklayer has a mate who mixes the mortar, and hauls it and water and bricks up to his boss, and while he does this he picks up the tricks of the trade and becomes a bricklayer in time, if he is clever.

All this may not seem difficult to you, but bricklaying is not all plain sailing. There are window and door openings to deal with, ventilators, string courses, cornices and special patterns in the brick, while building a chimney or a well-made arch is the work of a master. The essence of master bricklaying is to know the job so well that it goes on without interruption, smoothly and rapidly. A good 'bricky' can lay up to 1,000 bricks in a working day.

Carpenters and joiners are often spoken of together because they both deal with timber. Actually the carpenter does the rough work that seldom shows in the finished building, such as floors, roofs, rough lintels over doors and windows, and

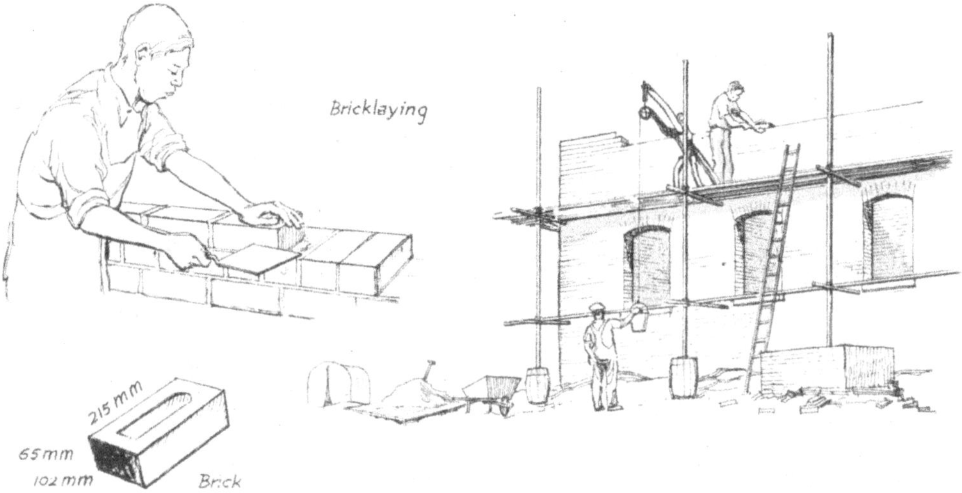

34 The unchanging craft of bricklaying, still the cheapest and the most suitable way of building for our English climate.

35 The old joiner's shop, smelling of sawdust and glue, is nearly gone, but so also is the quality of work that came from it.

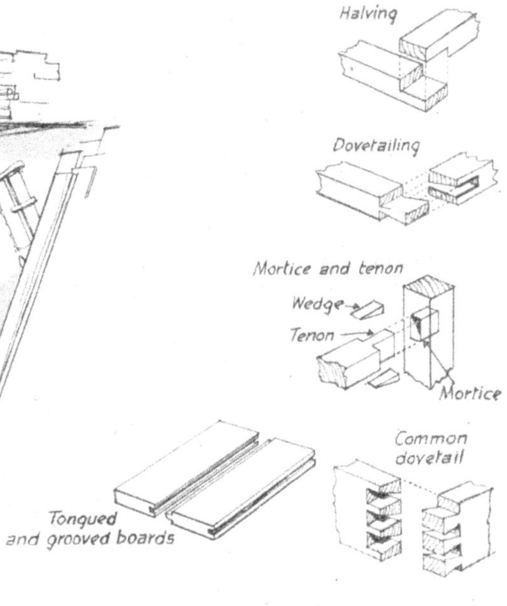

36 Some of the joints in wood, common to this type of workshop, which are now being replaced by machines.

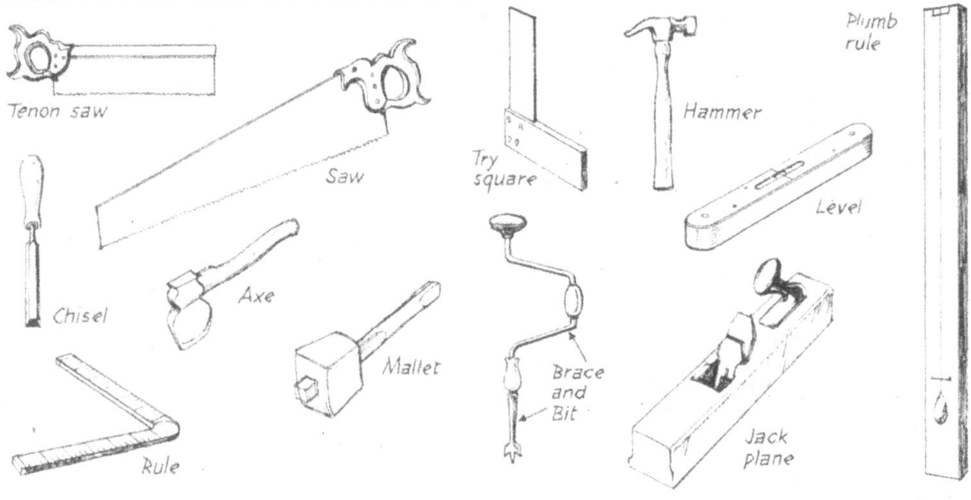

37 Carpenters' and joiners' hand tools, nearly all of which are still in use.

38 A section through a piece of veneered plywood showing how thin layers of wood, glued and pressed together, make an elegant but very strong material.

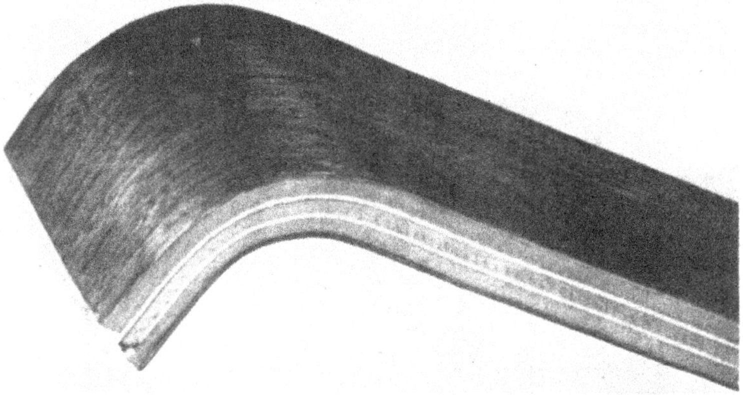

39 Chairs showing how plywood can be bent to form seat and back in one piece.

the boxes that are used to keep in concrete work until it has hardened. He works on the spot, and his principal tools are a good saw, a hammer and a box of nails. He does the rough stuff.

The joiner is a superior fellow who works at a bench in the builder's workshop, and his work is not taken to the job until it is nearly finished and needs only to be fitted into its place and neatened off. He uses a lot of tools: planes to smooth off his timber and bring it to the exact thickness; all kinds of chisels for cutting it, making holes for locks, for jointing one piece to another with mortice and tenon and other tricks of the trade, and for carving it when called for; braces and bits for boring holes; and several kinds of saw, all more delicate than those used by the carpenter. What a good place a joiner's shop used to be, smelling of shavings and hot glue and ringing with the blows of mallets and chisels and the loud noise of the saw!

We cannot describe everything the joiner does, because he does so many different things. He makes doors and windows, cupboards, staircases with lovely curling polished handrails, dressers, cabinets, sideboards and everything that is made of wood and fitted into the building. He works mostly in deal, a fairly cheap timber which generally comes from Russia and the Baltic countries and is usually painted, though quite often he uses harder and more beautiful woods such as oak, beech, walnut, mahogany, sycamore, and all manner of special veneers, which are thin sheets of lovely hardwood glued on to deal or other cheaper timber. Now he also has a great variety of plywoods, sheets of very thin wood in two, three, four or five layers glued or cemented together under great pressure. These sheets are always made with the grain of each sheet running counter to that of the next, and the finished sheet of ply is so hard that it plays havoc with saws and joiners' tempers. But we use it more and more, whatever the joiner cares to say about it.

Plywood is worth describing to you because it has brought many good changes into building. Veneers have been used for hundreds of years but are an expensive method of showing off the beauty of rare woods. It is only since we found the trick of shaving pieces off a whole log of wood that we have been able to make the plywood form of veneer cheaply. This is done by having a long sharp blade in a fixed position and rotating the log of wood, cutting off a miraculously thin, unbroken sheet, which is then flattened by steaming, cut into exact sizes and glued or cemented together under a large steel press.

Plywoods come to us from Finland, Russia, Scandinavia and Canada, and a few kinds are made in England, though too few to provide for more than a small fraction of our needs.

Also involved in putting up a building are the plumber and his mate with their blowlamp and their pot of boiling lead, bringing their pipes through unexpected holes and joining them to the right baths and basins. Then there are the smith, who deals with everything made in iron; the plasterer and the painter who come along when it is beginning to look like a building and fill the rooms with their singing and whistling; and the electrician, so often at odds with the bricklayer and the joiner because no one has left him holes to bring his wires through or blocks to fix his fittings to. By the time he comes on the job, to do his important work, nearly everyone is at it, hammering, sawing, smacking plaster on to walls, pulling wires through, and, because of the difference between one job and another, very much needing the guidance and good temper of the general foreman.

We have not spoken of the excavator and

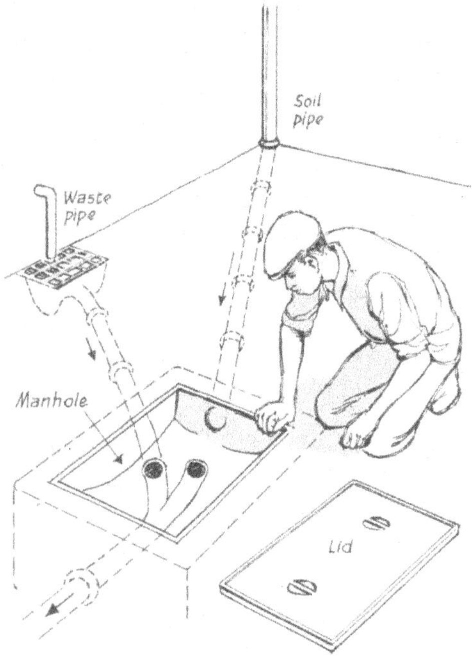

40 A drainlayer at work on a simple manhole taking the contents of house drains away to the sewer or septic tank.

concretor who start the job off, or of the drainlayer laying his pipes to fall gently but surely away, and gathering them together into little railway junctions that you will find if you get someone to lift one of the iron manhole covers you will most certainly find near your house. Nor have we mentioned the builder's labourer, that modest man of many trades who fetches and carries, does all kinds of rough work, holds the other end of the tape for the architect, and makes tea.

These are the men who on the normal small job do the work that one farmer–builder once took on his broad shoulders. Up to the nineteenth century, all work was done by such men (without the electrician, of course) and such tools. Medieval cathedrals, St Paul's, country houses and towns without number, farms and countless lesser work, saw groups of these skilful, modest men finding happiness in building.

With the nineteenth century England became a manufacturing country, its population increased at an unbelievable pace, and there was a demand for new kinds of building: for factories carrying heavy machinery on many floors; for bridges of wide spans and for enormous roofs to cover big railway stations. Brick could not do the job, as you may well imagine if you think of a brick arch the size of the roof of St Pancras Station. Brick was not strong enough to be used in the cotton mills, where big windows were needed to light the work inside. And so iron was developed on a new scale, first in the form of cast iron, which is heavy and brittle, and then as steel.

Steel is made from iron ore (haematite) and limestone heated together in a furnace. Steel is strong in every way. It will resist attempts to crush, pull or bend it. The limits of its strength are calculated so exactly that we know in advance how much steel to use and where to use it. At first steel was used only to make floors, but after a time we took to framing up the whole building. As the result was a rapidly constructed and immensely strong building, this method soon became common, especially in the United States of America, where they used it for their skyscrapers.

When a building is designed now the architect and the engineers work together and produce sets of drawings showing only the steelwork. These are sent to the steel rolling mills. With them goes an order for the exact amount of steel to be made and delivered to the building site ready for fixing, or the number and weight of steel bars to be embedded in concrete if the structure is to be of reinforced concrete. Other drawings show heating pipes, or electrical wires, etc. There is another, more complete set of drawings that show not only the steel, but the brick or other covering,

41 When steel is used the framework is erected first and clothed later.

and the windows, doors, plumbing and everything needed to make the final building. These are the architect's drawings.

When steel is used the framework for the complete job is erected first and then it is clothed with its brick or stone or concrete skin, and fitted inside and out in due course. You may have seen these steel skeletons going up. A large crane lifts each piece of steel into its proper place where men are waiting to bolt it fast or to weld it into position.

Steelwork has made a great revolution in building and changed its character almost completely, because where stone, brick and timber were heavy, steel building is light.

The second revolution came later with reinforced concrete, which we described to you briefly in the last chapter. Whereas steelwork is made up in the rolling mills and quickly erected on the building site, only the steel reinforcing rods are made in the steel mills, and when these come on site they have to be fixed very carefully at proper intervals before the wet concrete is run into the moulds. For every reinforced concrete

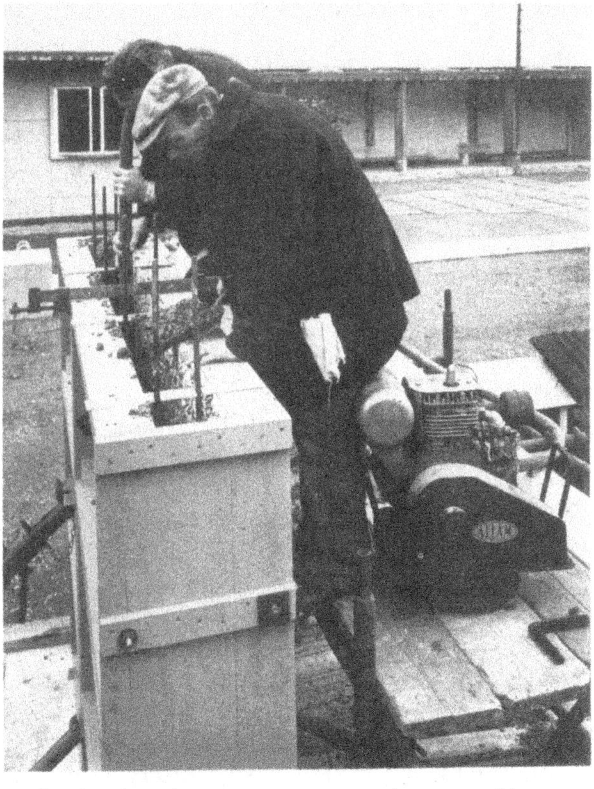

42 Steel rods and wet concrete are put into a mould to make a finished wall.

43 A handsome reinforced concrete bridge spanning the Yorkshire motorway and making a real contribution to the landscape. Scammonden Bridge.

column, beam, floor or wall there must be a mould to hold the concrete while it sets hard. These are built of rough carpenter's timber or re-usable sheets of thin steel. So there are three important things in this kind of construction – the moulds, the steel rods which are like bones inside the limbs of the building, and the concrete itself, poured wet into the moulds and shaken down with ramrods or 'punners' and sometimes with electric shakers or 'vibrators' fixed to the moulds.

It sounds more complicated than it really is, for when the mould forms are taken off or 'struck', as we say, the complete framework and many of the walls are finished, fireproof and nearly bombproof, with all holes for pipes and lifts and windows left ready.

What steel will do, reinforced concrete will do nearly equally well, and both are used for the same kind of buildings. It is only when we come to build really high skyscrapers and giant bridges such as the Severn Bridge, that steel is definitely superior, and of course, it is the best material for big ships.

Building is no longer the straightforward business it used to be, and we have all become used to the comforts and luxuries that machinery brings. However much we may admire the sweet simplicity of the country cottage, we should be dismayed if our ceilings were to be lowered to within a few inches of our heads, if the windows were to shrink to a quarter of their size, if bathrooms and w.c.s disappeared and with them the water. We are used to our luxuries; they have become necessities.

Behind all these things that we have come to accept is a world of machinery and factory production without which you could not have your hot bath, or your cold drink from the refrigerator, or your late cup of cocoa heated on the gas cooker; nor could you switch on the instantaneous electric light, or hop on your bicycle or a bus. So you might as well know something about the machines that make your buildings and are fitted into them.

The machines that are used in building need not worry you much. These are the ugly creatures on caterpillar tracks that excavate the ground, and cranes of all sizes. You have all seen the pneumatic hammers that make such a din in the road. They make just as much din on a building, but they do the work of five men who make a lesser din for a longer time. So do such things as electric grinders for smoothing stonework and concrete, or floor smoothers and polishers and paint sprays. These things only do work more quickly, not differently. The mechanical concrete mixer does no more than this, but without it reinforced concrete building would be next to impossible and it is therefore the commonest and the most useful machine in building.

We must tell you of some of the changes that have visited the builder's joinery workshop and made something of a factory of it. It is still a very pleasant place, but the irregular sounds of mallet, chisel and saw are now drowned by the whine of machinery – the circular bandsaw tearing through timber as though it were currant cake, mechanical planers taking in rough boards and getting them nearly as smooth as a man with a hand-plane would, chain-morticing machines that cut holes for locks in seconds instead of minutes, and the whizzing spindle that shapes wood as though it were a magician rather than a machine tool. A new power has come to the joiner's shop and it breeds a new skill. We, personally, like it less than the old, having known both, but if we were as young as you are and came fresh to these workshops, as we hope you will, we think we should find them as fascinating and as full of life and skill as ever we found the old.

The machinery that goes into the building is much more important. Few people care to walk up more than four flights of stairs without a good rest between flights, so that without lifts most of our larger buildings would be unusable, the New York skyscrapers would never have been attempted, and the deep London tube would be impossible. The lift is the most spectacular of the machines used in building, but if you are ever taken round a large office building, or a hospital, or a theatre or large cinema, you will be impressed by the huge boilers that provide the heating and hot water. Once upon a time they were looked after by a stoker who shovelled and sweated in a dirty pair of pants and singlet from morning to night. But now he looks after a mechanical stoker, or a set of oil jets, and is more of an engineer than a stoker. He is also a good deal cooler and cleaner.

Heating systems are based on the simple fact that hot water, like hot air, rises. Therefore you find that the furnace and boiler are in the kitchen or the basement in your house, and are always in the basement in other buildings. Water is brought to the boil in the boiler and overflows upward at once into a cylinder near by and makes room for colder water to flow into the boiler to be boiled.

If cold water was brought directly to the boiler next to the fire, there would be trouble. So a pipe is brought back from the bottom of the cooler end of the cylinder to the boiler, and round and round goes the water, rushing boiling hot up the pipe from the boiler into the cylinder and falling back slightly cooler into the boiler again. The water at the top of the cylinder is pretty hot and a pipe goes from the top to the top of the house, where there is an overflow in case of real trouble. From there the hot water drops down to feed the bathroom – bath and basin and the towel rail, perhaps a radiator or two, and the linen cupboard, and then down again to the kitchen sink, and the cloakroom, and so into the pipe that leads back to the boiler. It is really a simple idea that works like clockwork in most houses, but it will not work so well in large buildings because of the distances the water has to travel. In big heating and hot water schemes, therefore, the water is helped on its way by a pump. That is the only difference: that and the size of the thing. We now provide hot water for whole towns more cheaply than we can do for individual buildings. Thamesmead is served in this way.

Inside the cistern over or behind the w.c. you will find a simple little machine called a ball valve. This is a sort of automatic hand: it turns the water on when the ball that floats on the top of the water is lowered (as the water flows out of the cistern into the bowl below), and shuts it off as the water level rises to the top again. There is another ball valve in the storage cistern under the roof. We could go on to tell you about all kinds of complicated machinery that is fitted to large buildings such as theatres, cinemas, hospitals, factories and so on, but we don't want to bore you with too much technical talk, and none of these things affect buildings as much as the things we have already discussed.

It is the introduction of new materials and forms of construction and the rapid development of some of the older materials that have so changed the character of architecture. We have already spoken about steel and concrete, but have you ever thought of the changes that have taken place in the making of glass? In the seventeenth century the biggest size of window glass you could get was about eight inches in the longest direction. This size was governed by what could be cut from a disc of glass blown out of an iron tube by a glass-blower and twisted over the furnace. The glass made by this method was clear and brilliant, but showed the twist mark and distorted whatever was seen through it. Today plate glass is made in sheets that are thirty to forty times as long as the seventeenth-century size, are dead flat, highly polished and give a clear and accurate vision. Plate glass is the luxury glass, but normal sheet glass, made by the mile in great automatic machines, is as accurate as plate glass used to be and a lot cheaper. In the glass-works at St Helens, Lancashire, which have been working since the seventeenth century, they show you how glass used to be blown with great labour, men heaving and sweating through long days of toil before furnaces, blowing their insides out and drinking large draughts of beer to cool their throats. Now the furnaces are even hotter, but they are nearly out of sight, for glass-making is more scientific, more mechanical, and the skilled men are supervisors and engineers rather than toilers.

The introduction of large sheets of glass into building was first seen in shop windows, when shopkeepers took out their old smaller windows, and regardless of the total effect, put in long lines of plate glass windows through which the public could see a vast array of goods. It looked rather silly, of course, to see a heavy building standing on plate glass, and correct-minded architects and others thought that the end of architecture had come. They were very shocked.

It was in fact the beginning of a new architecture in which steel, concrete and glass took the place of stone, brick and timber, and we now enjoy its elegance and lightness as seen from the outside, and the sun and air that it gives us inside the building.

The latest developments in glass-making have produced glass bricks, strong enough to be built into large walls of translucent light, a very beautiful conception; armoured glass, which is nearly unbreakable; 'vita' glass, which allows the health-giving ultra-violet rays to pass through; and opaque glasses of many lovely colours. Each of these has a special function to perform in modern architecture.

Glass is an old material that science has improved, but the range of materials known

44 The Glass Museum at Pilkington's, St Helens, is entirely lined with glass: windows, walls and fascia.

as plastics, the outcome of the science of organic chemistry – the chemistry of living organisms – is entirely new. The earliest form, and almost the only form of it from about 1870 until recent years, was xylonite, made from rubber. This is the black stuff used for fountain pens, bicycle pumps etc.

Modern plastics range from the transparent to the opaque, and are very varied in their properties. Some melt with heat, others do not, some are better for moulding, others better in sheet form, some take colours without fading – they have a great variety of useful properties.

When you know that boats, cars and planes are made of plastics; when you realise how many articles of daily use in the house and in building – the door-knobs, electrical fittings, kitchen and bathroom fittings, etc. – are made from one or another type of plastic, you will not be surprised to find it taking quite an important part in the building of the future.

The old way of making things was to make each thing in the particular way it was wanted, and as long as everything was hand-made there was no reason why each customer should not please himself. Even then the amount of variety was not very great because so many people want the same things and follow custom and fashion as being the easiest thing to do.

The industrial or factory way of working is exactly the opposite. It is based on the assumption that most people want the same things, and that those who want something different can pay for it to be different.

This is a quite reasonable assumption for most of the articles needed in building. The person who wants a bath 1 metre wide and

3 metres long obviously doesn't mind having to heat all the water required to fill the bath, and is a rarity. Most people are quite happy with a normal-sized bath, a normal-sized basin, normally wide doors and normally high windows – normal people, in fact, being about the same height and weight, and having to live the same life, with its round of eating, sleeping, washing, etc., have a steady need for a range of normally sized equipment.

A machine is a device for performing over and over again one or several actions that would otherwise be done by a man, or several men, working together. A machine will only do the one thing or series of things it is designed to do, and the costs of designing and making a machine are very heavy. Before making one, therefore, it is necessary to know whether what it is to make is needed by a lot of people, for once started the machine must work continuously and long and produce an enormous number of copies of the model article or standard pattern it works to.

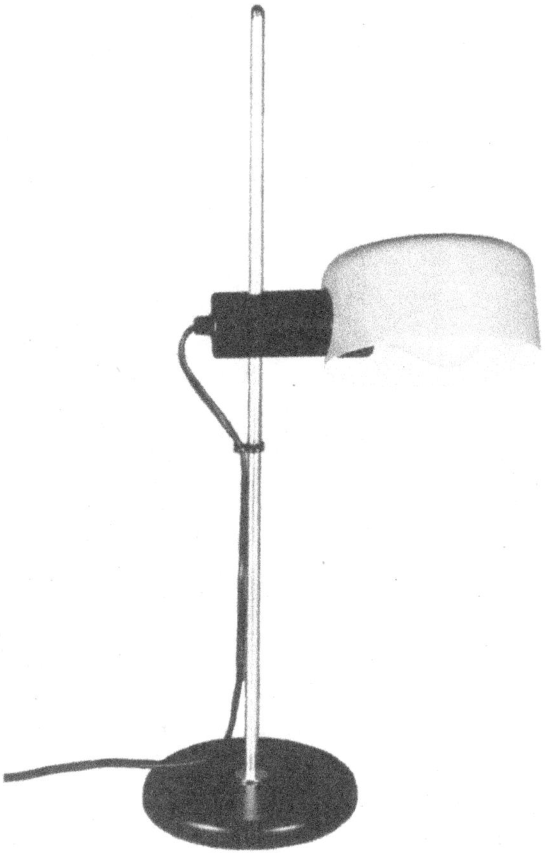

46 A really adaptable light fitting that belongs to our time.

45 Steel tubes, moulded sponge rubber and man-made fibre covering compose a new elegance for the modern home.

This system of standardisation and mass production has created an entirely new kind of product, beautiful in its way, different from the old hand-made article, cleaner in outline and with smoother surfaces. This characteristic cleanness of line and smoothness of surface is often called streamlining, but this is nonsense. Only a few things like aeroplanes, cars and locomotives are designed to minimise the pressure of air, producing this effect of streamlining; in all other products of the machine the smooth appearance comes from pressing sheet metal into the various parts.

The effect of working to a selected number

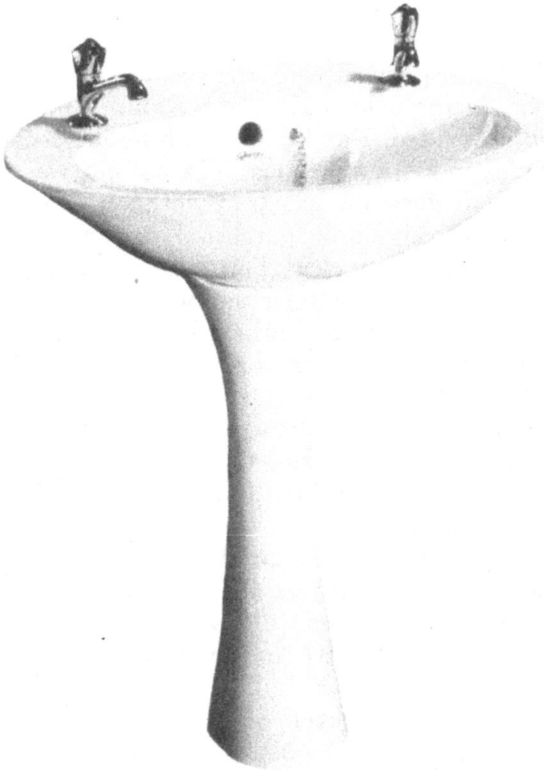

47 The beauty of this wash-basin is no accident. It is a good example of art applied to industry.

of standards for normal needs and mass-producing articles in great numbers is to bring their prices down to the income levels of ordinary people. Motor-cars, refrigerators, vacuum cleaners, gramophones, radios and television sets, all of them at one time rich men's toys, are now in common use. And do not forget that baths and fireplaces, plumbing systems and drains, metal windows and spring-beds were all luxury articles in the days when everything was made by hand.

As this system of mass production developed it had an extraordinary effect on building. When we drew the picture of a group of men working on the building of a small house, we tried to give you the impression of a building being made either on the site or in the joiner's shop; of timber being cut to lengths and fitted in, of doors and windows being made on the benches of the joiner's shop, of plumbers and smiths making this thing, and that, and themselves fixing them into the building.

That way of working is vanishing under pressure of the industrial system. If we were to give you a list of all the parts of a building, from steel framework to door-knobs, that are completed in the factory and brought on to the job, it would fill the rest of the book. A building today is an assembly of standard factory articles, which would be a regrettable fact were it not that the majority of these factory-made things are of good and lasting

48 A whole dwelling unit being hoisted into position at the famous Habitat '67 housing scheme at the '67 Exhibition at Montreal.

quality and excellent design. An old craftsman skill is disappearing. A new skill is taking its place.

As time goes on the tendency will be to make larger and larger parts of buildings in the factory where the work can be economically organised under cover, and eventually, following the example of the motor-car and the aeroplane, to make complete houses or parts of houses in the factory and transport them fully finished to a selected site. This is happening and with it the need for much more careful planning of towns. We cannot leave such important matters as these in the hands of commercial men whose main concern is profit rather than the environment, and we rather fancy that as building becomes even more a matter of machinery, it will be even more controlled for us by local authorities and the State. This change would not be so noticeable as one might think, because building is already controlled by the very big firms and financiers who own most of the expensive machines.

You have now heard of three systems of building. The first was represented by the farmer–builder of the fifteenth century who found his materials, with the smallest exceptions, in the fields and woods around him, and provided the labour – himself, his family and a few helpers. The second was represented by the group of workmen with their relatively simple hand-tools and tackle, who made nearly every part of the building on the site or in their homely builders' workshop, a way of working that persisted for hundreds of years and is only now giving way to a third system, in which the machine is the chief instrument, the factory the builders' workshop, and the site little more than the assembly platform for what is already done.

These are great changes that require to be understood clearly by us all if we are to get the best from them. When you have read the rest of the book and have an idea of the size of the task of continued building and rebuilding that faces us everywhere, you will see perhaps that it will not be done without a very full use of the machine and the factory.

49 A great modern interior of reinforced concrete and glass at the Crystal Palace Sports Centre, London.

5
The Art of Architecture

There is some dispute today as to whether architecture is an art of just a way of assembling things that a computer might do equally well. Doubts of this sort come naturally to an age that relies so much upon machines, factories and electronic instruments, although it is in just such an age that the *art* of doing things as opposed to the *mechanism* of doing them becomes doubly important.

Much of the damage done to our environment arises from the necessity and the habit of specialisation; of doing things, and mainly scientific and industrial things, in watertight compartments with little thought of what is going on elsewhere.

It is difficult to avoid specialisation. We owe a great deal to the care with which specialists pursue their particular interests knowing that science is so many-sided that a person's whole life can be absorbed in the study of something that is only a small part of the whole.

Out of this have come inventions and processes of the greatest usefulness, and in the building industry an endless flood of appliances, machines, factory-made components, systems of building, even whole house units.

It is bewildering in its variety. It is chaotic. And in general it is commercial and the craftsmen are replaced, though not yet entirely, by the factory workers.

Building as we have described it in earlier chapters has become much more a matter of assembling factory units on the building site, and though this has its skills, they are largely specialist ones.

Now if building were to become entirely a matter of factory production and assembly the outlook would be bleak. Already we feel the pressure of the machine and the machine-mind in our cities and when we find them cold and forbidding, when building seems to us to lack the human touch, the warmth that invests old buildings, we are unconsciously voicing the need in our life for art.

Art is difficult to define. At the upper levels you have great artists – painters, writers, musicians, architects – producing works of lasting value, which sooner or later are universally acclaimed. At the lower levels you have craftsmen in great variety whose products are works of art in their own right.

And, still at this lower end, you have classes of building all over the world which, like our yeoman farmer's house, have no claims to be regarded as architecture and yet are beautiful.

There must be something that connects these various classes of work, or artefacts, as we sometimes call them, and if we could put it in a single word it would be 'wholeness'. It is easy to imagine an artist such as Gainsborough pouring himself into a canvas so that it became not only a direct reflection of himself but of the eighteenth century to which he belonged.

It is not difficult to see how a craftsman working on natural materials puts his whole personality into the task of transforming wood and metal into useful or decorative articles that have the ring of truth about them, and the shapeliness that is an aspect of all art.

One can understand how the design of a yacht or an aeroplane, which involves a lot of people besides the designer, is nevertheless a very direct collaboration between the forces of nature, in the form of winds, water and air; the materials that will withstand their heavy demands; and the imagination of a designer at full stretch co-ordinating these many factors into one unifying object.

But the last class of building, which no one seems to have designed, is more difficult to explain. It is usually simple, though some African *kraals* are as intricate as a shell. It draws its purpose from well-understood social needs for shelter for man, his animals and his food. It draws its materials from those nearest to hand. But finally it is a process repeated over long periods of time, again and again and again, until everything that has to do with it has sunk into the minds of the people involved, who are usually both builders and users.

In this way direct contact and long usage correspond to the more vivid imagination needed to absorb all that bears on the creation of a work of art: it is a matter of time.

So when we come to consider the art of building, which is architecture, and the art of organising large groups of buildings into towns and cities, which is an extension of architecture into town planning, we see a great variety of materials and components. Some are still natural, such as wood and stone. Some are semi-natural, such as bricks, which are clay moulded and burnt into a state of permanent hardness. Very many are synthetic and either rely on their appearance, or try to look like natural materials, and usually fail; still more are manufactured ready to use in building, or as a finished product.

Our lives have become many-sided and lack the accepted customs and shared opinions of former times. We are constantly excited by the mass media – television and

50 A VC10. An aeroplane is a work of complicated technology involving many men and machines. It is also an intense collaboration between man and the forces of nature. Finally it is a work of the imagination, for behind every great plane there is the individual mind of a designer co-ordinating everything.

radio, newspapers and magazines – to want new things and new outlets. But we do not and perhaps cannot give ourselves enough time to allow things to work out. Therefore we need people who have the imagination to be able to co-ordinate our requirements and the manifold materials available and transform them into the buildings and landscape that will make up our future environment.

Somewhere in this hurly-burly there must be someone who, slightly disconnected from the market-place of affairs, will consider not only immediate needs and the latest gadgets, but the real needs, the structures and buildings appropriate to them, and their continuation well into the future.

In the world of building this kind of person is called an architect, and he, or she, is more than an executant, more even than a co-ordinator: he is essentially creative; he is an artist.

His problems are always practical and can be stated quite simply as follows:

(*a*) there is a need for some activity to be sheltered.

(*b*) how to do it? With what materials and structures best suited to the need?

(*c*) how much will it cost?

(*d*) how long will it take to do?

These general considerations apply to all work from a single dwelling to a large complex of buildings such as a university, or a city even.

But the needs vary. They were once simple, traditional and understood by everyone concerned. They have become complicated as society has multiplied its activities. They involve more people as population increases. They become less well understood as scientific techniques become more elaborate.

Nevertheless they remain as the needs which architects must cater for and therefore come to understand. Thus the first thing required of an architect is that he should understand and sympathise with the world he lives in, should know something of how it came about and in what direction it is moving.

How to do the job is the architect's dominant problem. Up to the beginning of the nineteenth century it was never acute because the means of building were obvious and, except for unusual buildings, could be obtained locally. What gave such character to all earlier building, and particularly to the class of anonymous building we have mentioned, was the universal use of whatever natural materials lay at hand, for these dictated the kind of structures best suited to them.

Our machine civilisation has multiplied the choice of materials, and with the invention of steel and reinforced concrete, of structures too. Not only has it mechanised the products and the building site, but it has brought machines into buildings as permanent installations without which they cannot function. You have only to think of lifts, and air-conditioning, or to glance at your refrigerator or heating system, to see how true this is.

There is one mercy granted to an architect, which is that in any one building he can only have one structural system, one heating or air-conditioning system: only one of all the many alternatives offered to him. But he must make an early choice, guided by his knowledge and experience. Sometimes, indeed, there is no obvious alternative; and sometimes he will experiment without full knowledge and experience of what he is about, and take the consequences, which may be severe.

He makes his choice in company with many others with the same problems to solve, using the experience of others whose works he sees and judges, and with some backing of custom and tradition, though this is not so strong now as it was in the past.

His choice is influenced by the considerations of what materials and structure are most suited to the work, what they will cost to build and to maintain in the future, and how long it will all take.

When, years ago, we started building large schools in Ghana and Nigeria, these were difficult problems to solve. There were no bricks, and though there was wood in plenty it got eaten by white ants. There was hardly any architecture except mud huts to go on; building was rudimentary; builders were unorganised and unused to large contracts; and the work was scattered all over a large country.

The climate was most difficult: wet, humid, and with big variations in temperature. The sun, when it was not hidden by clouds, was tropical and fierce, the rain torrential. With no air-conditioning to rely upon, the problem of keeping reasonably cool could only be solved by allowing the fairly constant breeze to pass over people's bodies when in the shade: it meant an architecture only one room thick with plenty of air moving across it.

And it meant, we decided, walls that were screens that would let the air through, roofs that lay east and west where possible so that the sun would travel over them rather than on to them, and roofs that would not heat up too much in the day and would give their heat up quickly in the night.

We would make our structures of reinforced concrete, our walls of perforated blocks, and our roofs of light asbestos sheet easily transported and erected. We would use stone where we could find it, and colour wherever it showed to advantage. And so, largely influenced by climate, we made an architecture that has since been accepted as being the architecture of the humid tropics. Its basis was severely practical, but its final

51 Sunbreaker horizontal louvres keep sun off the windows and allow heat to disperse upwards so that cool air passes into the building. A science block in a school in Ghana.

appearance was a work of architectural imagination.

By contrast, but on the same theme, a group of young architects in Hertfordshire were faced with the problem of building a lot of schools at a time after the Second World War when there were few bricklayers and carpenters, little money to spare, and an urgent need to fulfil.

They faced a different problem from ours and they solved it differently. Having no bricklayers or carpenters they analysed their school building problem and found that it had many repeating elements, of classroom sizes, doors and windows, lavatories etc. Out of their findings they evolved a system of building in which the standard parts could be made in a factory and bolted up quickly on the site; and this they did so cleverly and with such an eye to good proportions and convenience, using colour

52 The large library of Ibadan University, Nigeria, where an equable interior climate, free of insects, is maintained by several devices which contribute to the character of the architecture.

53 Aboyne Lodge Infants School, St Albans, Herts. One of the first prefabricated schools in England and a beautiful example of art directing industry.

to bring out the various parts and add gaiety to the whole, that they revolutionised school building by showing that industrialised building could be beautiful in its own right, as human as any other, and cheaper.

The problem that faced these young men then has become more acute with time because there are so many more people in need of schools and dwellings, shops and all the other buildings that make up our environment. While on the other hand, with high wages and inflation and the reluctance of men to use their hands when machines can do the work more easily, there are fewer craftsmen with traditional experience, though bricklaying is still a strong trade and good bricks are available at a price.

What we need is an architecture that makes the best of what is offered – machine-made products, reinforced concrete, which is so adaptable, and the traditional materials such as wood and bricks that are still available. To this end we must set greater value than we do on the creative side of architecture and the workings of the imagination, and we must learn to honour and respect fine architecture when we see it; that of our own time no less than that of the past.

The problems we have described are not only practical. When an architect assembles the multiple purposes and means of building into a work of architecture he is transforming dead matter into a living work of art that not only makes manifest the purpose it was designed for, but has qualities that we recognise as lying above and beyond the immediate needs that brought it about and that speak to us of proportions, of contrasts of light, shade and texture, and the passage of time. Drama speaks to us of passion; painting of the lasting beauties of the physical world and the animal world. Architecture speaks to us of the more slow-moving, deep-seated emotions connected with light and shade, mass and contrast, but speak it must, or it is not architecture.

There are three stages in the creative process of architecture, apart from the constant process of observation and comparison that goes on throughout an architect's life.

The first stage, once the architect has been given a commission, is one of weighing up the brief. He receives a set of instructions, which may be fairly exact only if they are for a known type of building like a school or an office; a site to build on; and often a sum of money to spend or to aim at. This is a stage of fairly cool analysis, of reducing things to some order while looking for a guiding system, and of calculating size against cost. From this first stage emerge decisions on the basis of 'you can't do this, and you can't do that, but you might do something else'. These decisions are forced on the architect by the nature of the site, by cost and time, factors that incline him first this way and then that until he finds himself merging into the second stage where the struggle with facts and figures gives way to something that is not a struggle but a release.

This second stage is a mystery. How it happens no one really knows. But in it the whole assembly of facts, figures, sizes, movements, the whole of everything bearing on the problem is fused into one unified scheme of things which is the design, simple or complicated, but the solution of all the problems in one.

Out of this often fierce concentration of thought come new form, new invention, and new beauty that carry our civilisation a step forward, though the immediate aim is to perform a practical service to the present time.

The third stage is the preparation of working or construction drawings with detailed instructions on how the various trades must co-operate to produce the finished building. This is a laborious and painstaking task, with much correction and detailed fitting-in of intricate parts, and pricing and re-pricing, but one in which the true character of the building is stamped on every link.

This process, or something like it, obtains over the whole field of design, for small buildings and great, for houses and for cities.

The architect even as an architect–planner fades out at the level of a town or city, but at this stage the process is very similar.

A city consists of four major elements: living, or where and how people live, which occupies 80 per cent of the space of most cities; working, or where and how people work in both large and small industries; recreation, or how people recreate themselves by sport, learning in schools or colleges, relaxing in good surroundings; and communication, or how and in what way they get from one place to another, a problem that has got out of proportion due to the motor-car.

Since the eighteenth century these things had never been considered. Up to that time there were quite definite market towns, great and small, from Chipping Campden to Norwich. There were cultural towns like Oxford and Cambridge, quiet centres of learning. There were health and pleasure towns like Bath, Cheltenham and Brighton. Each had its distinct character and form, and each was in its way a work of art, conceived as such or made so by slow time.

Since the last war we in Britain have tried to make up for the mistakes of the past by designing and building more than thirty new towns, in each of which we have tried to solve the problems in the way we have described: choosing sites in useful positions, then making designs that allot space for each of the three functions, tied together by the last one by railway, road, cycle-path and footpath.

The conscious aim of these towns has been, and is, to create a good human environment in which there is a balance in favour of living, in which natural form in trees, grass and flowers delights our eyes, and in which useless travel and dangerous travel are

54 The market town of Chipping Campden, built up slowly over the centuries in the stone of the region.

55 The miraculous health and pleasure town of Bath, conceived as a single work of art that reflected the culture of eighteenth-century England. The Royal Crescent is in the foreground.

56 (*opposite, top*) Motorway madness at the 'spaghetti junction' of the M5 and M6. We must control this monster before it controls us.

57 (*opposite, bottom*) Runcorn. The centre of the town is a covered shopping centre to which all traffic converges, with cars separated from public transport.

reduced to the minimum.

Some of these towns are based on neighbourhoods grouped round schools, churches and little shopping centres, others bring people by rapid bus and car routes to a single centre. In some there are highly developed cycle- and footpaths moving independently of the roads, and each town strives in one way or another to solve the problems of modern living, of which by far the most difficult is the accommodation of the private motor-car.

This terribly space-taking vehicle, which offers freedom and gives status, is throttling us. It started as a benefit and is becoming a curse because it takes up so much room, either moving or standing. We must limit the total number of cars for the country or face stagnation, which is utter pollution, and the destruction of both town and country. It stares us in the face and you will be called upon to make up your minds about it in the near future.

Meanwhile it makes every kind of planning that much more difficult and forces us to choose between private or public transport, between walking a bit and waiting a bit in conditions of relative peace and quiet, or continuing the rat race to the bitter end.

In new towns such as Runcorn and Thamesmead there is an attempt to strike a balance in favour of public transport. In the new capital city of Brasilia the motor-car triumphs as it does in Los Angeles where the giant motorways coil like serpents over and through a formless landscape of development.

There are schemes to create great linear cities based on giant motorways with the country on each side preserved, such as are to be found in Poland. There have been

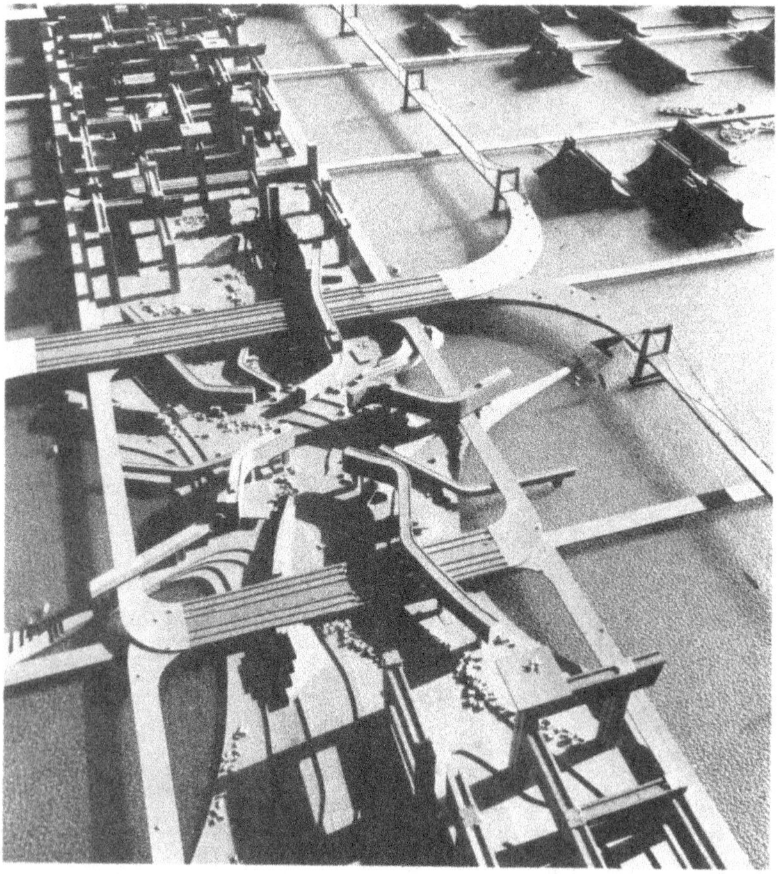

58 (*above*) The air-conditioned shopping centre at Runcorn, reached without fatigue or danger.

59 (*left*) A Japanese project to extend bursting Tokyo over the waters of the bay: a desperate remedy for a desperate situation.

60 (*right*) The French city of Toulouse le Mirail, which tries to separate cars from pedestrians and preserve open space for communal use.

61 Sheffield, once the world's workshop, was an insult to man and nature as it fouled the valleys and polluted the streams.

62 New Sheffield rises on the hilltops above newly created open space, while the valleys are being rebuilt and parklands penetrate the city from the moors above.

fantastic structures evolved by the Japanese to solve the horrifying congestion of Tokyo, which has grown into a city of 20 millions. The French are experimenting with new city forms that separate traffic from people, spurred on by their great prophet–architect Le Corbusier.

All these demonstrate the real extent of the jam we have got ourselves into with rising populations and technocratic solutions, of which the motor-car is the worst example, with the aeroplane coming next.

On top of all this comes the realisation of pollution. In Wordsworth's noble words:

The world is too much with us; late and soon,
Getting and spending, we lay waste our powers:
Little we see in Nature that is ours;
We have given our hearts away, a sordid boon!

That is what has happened to our world, too clever, too self-centred, too greedy. And now our chief task is to come to new terms with the wonderful natural world we inhabit, this thin skin of land and water on the turning globe which we have so maltreated and exploited, but on which we still hope to lead purposeful and, if possible, peaceful lives.

6 How our Forefathers Built

Having read the rest of the book you will find it easier to appreciate architecture, knowing that it goes with the sort of life lived by those who built it – their life, their skill, the inventions they made to overcome their difficulties, the materials they could lay their hands on, their religion and their memory.

As life changes so does architecture, and as life varies from one district and country to another, so is architecture infinitely variable. The history of architecture is a history of the changing lives of nations, a history more accurate than the normal history book which often lays too much stress upon the doings of warriors and kings, and too little upon the day-to-day lives of the people themselves.

This history goes back into the furthest recesses of time when all we know about races of people who must have lived and thrived over periods as long as and longer than our own Western civilisation is to be learnt from the remains of their religious architecture. Stonehenge is a temple of sorts; some say that it was a temple to the sun, and there is a theory that connects it with Egypt. Nobody knows for certain, and the architecture is the only record of a race that has faded from memory.

Memory plays an important part in architecture because people do not wish to work the thing out for themselves if they can remember how someone else did it, or if they have an actual example before their eyes. It is therefore interesting in looking at architecture to know something of the long history of its development through the ages and how one type or style of architecture led to another.

For our Western civilisation up to recent years the fountain of architecture has been Greece and Rome; but behind Greece stands Egypt, where great races of peoples lived along the fertile valley of the Nile for thousands of years before Christianity. It is unnecessary to go further back, for whether or not the Egyptians borrowed ideas from other still older races, it was they who worked out an architecture impressive enough to affect those who came after them in the Mediterranean world.

The Egyptians' lives were dominated by two things – the sun and the Nile – for with the combination of water and sun they grew their corn and became powerful. To worship the sun and the river was natural and necessary, as was the rule of their priests, the chief among whom was also their king. These priest-kings, being regarded as gods, were

63 The temple of the Egyptian goddess Isis at Philae, built for eternity to commemorate the lives of absolute rulers.

entirely powerful and in command of numberless slaves. We know very little of how the slaves and common people lived. Their dwellings were probably of timber and clay or mud and have vanished utterly. Only the tombs and temples remain, but these are so vast, and so solidly built of such great stones that they have been little touched by time, and tell us clearly what kind of people these priest-kings were, and how preoccupied with the idea of eternal life.

The pyramids were tombs of stone in the centre of which lay the bodies of kings and queens preserved in wrappings and spices so as to last for ever: these tombs are dead things. The Sphinx is a temple or a monument, the meaning of which will remain a mystery for us for all time: it tells us nothing. But from the temples, with their dim forests of giant lotus-headed columns, barring the way to the inner sanctuaries of the priest myth, springs the whole world of classic architecture, for in these mysterious and impressive buildings the simple idea of the post and lintel was first clothed and given form and grandeur in solid stone. Whatever may have been built in less lasting materials, by whatever tribes and peoples inhabiting the other shores of the Mediterranean, must yield to the achievement of the Pharaohs: this is the source.

The next memorable civilisation flourished in the Grecian Archipelago and along the shores of Asia Minor – as the result of maritime trading combined with war. This region was the centre of the then known world, and the opportunity for trade and wealth which this position gave to the various tribes and clans who occupied it united them in a commonwealth of States. They became extremely wealthy, and so well secured in their dominant position that they found time to cultivate science, philosophy and art.

It is useful to remember that every civil-

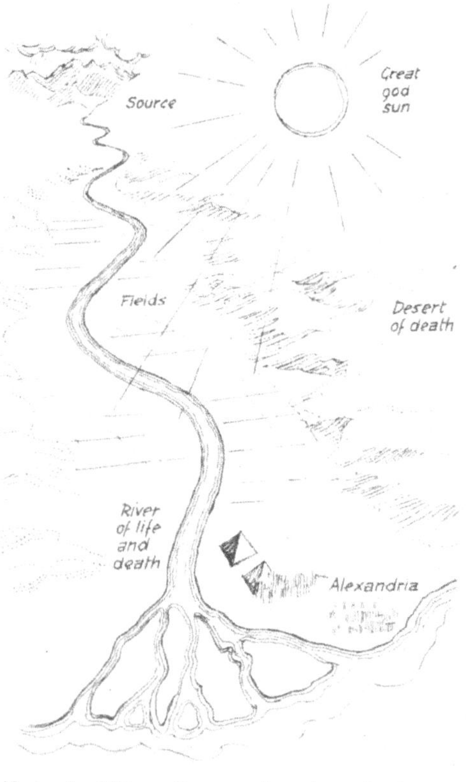

64 Life in the Nile valley was based on the hard facts of nature – sun, river and desert. Their interpretation through science and art created the most enduring civilisation known to us.

isation is the result of circumstances. The Egyptians did not make their civilisation; it arose because the Nile was the most fertile place in the known world, and attracted people to it. As the world, which was then the Mediterranean world, grew larger, Greece became its centre. Egypt continued, but Greece flourished and attracted life to it.

The trade and successful conquests of the Greeks could be carried out without making one powerful State of them, and so they preserved the idea of local independence and a system of government in which many people shared. Their religion set great value on beautiful living, did not prevent free thought and discussion, and was itself a very lovely allegory or story explanation of the meaning of life.

The architecture of Greece added no new inventions of any importance. It was an architecture of post and lintel, built in stone and marble, but of a richness and beauty never excelled either before or since. Though based on the simplest constructional system, it suited their religious and secular purposes. In the early period it was severe, and grew softer, richer and subtler as one generation of artists after another, sharing in the fruitful life of this race of philosophers, scientists and poets, set their hands to the familiar task. Simple though these temples are in general conception – a single or a double cell housing the statue of the god, surrounded by one or two rows of columns carrying the flat-pitched roof – they were built to the highest degree of accuracy in the finest marble, immaculately proportioned and decorated in low relief, sometimes coloured, by the best artists.

The important items of Greek architecture are the column with its base and its capital; the beam, or entablature above it; and the projection of the roof, or cornice. They may have grown from a wooden architecture because the divisions of the various members have a slight suggestion of timber construction. But that is no longer of importance compared with the beauty of the buildings in which these simple elements were used.

65 One of the most beautiful examples of the Doric style: a reconstruction of the Parthenon at Athens, showing how it may have looked.

You will find examples of the three types of columns developed independently of each other in various parts of the commonwealth. The Doric remains throughout severe, relying entirely upon proportion and colour. The Ionic is graceful and very delicate. And the Corinthian is rich, abundant and intricate in design.

Besides temples the Greeks built tombs and memorials of varied shapes, and open-air theatres and games stadia. The houses and towns, ports and warehouses, which were indispensable to a trading nation, are gone; only the temples remain; but from them we are able to understand why Greek art and thought have lived on in men's memories to the present day.

As the countries round the Mediterranean came into contact with each other, trade expanded and finally moved its centre to Italy. Greece in the meantime had wasted its wealth and undermined its culture by large-scale wars extending as far as India.

The Romans were even more warlike than the Greeks, intensely practical, hard-

66 The Acropolis at Athens is the religious monument of a civilisation that has fertilised the Western world.

headed, disciplined and with a flair for organisation. To balance this they were unoriginal in their thinking, borrowing from the Greeks their religion, philosophy, science and art.

They never approached the levels of Greek art, but as they had quite different problems to tackle their contribution was of another kind. At home, for instance, they had to build buildings to house enormous crowds. Rome had well over a million inhabitants. This great troublesome population needed water and it needed keeping quiet by distractions such as sport, public baths, and religious and warlike demonstrations. Covered spaces such as the Greeks never dreamt of were required to house these multitudes, and feats of engineering to bring

67 Post and lintel construction was limited by the size of a single stone. The Roman invention of the arch freed architecture for use and display. The result: water for the Roman city, roads across the Empire.

68 The Pont du Gard, Nîmes, France.

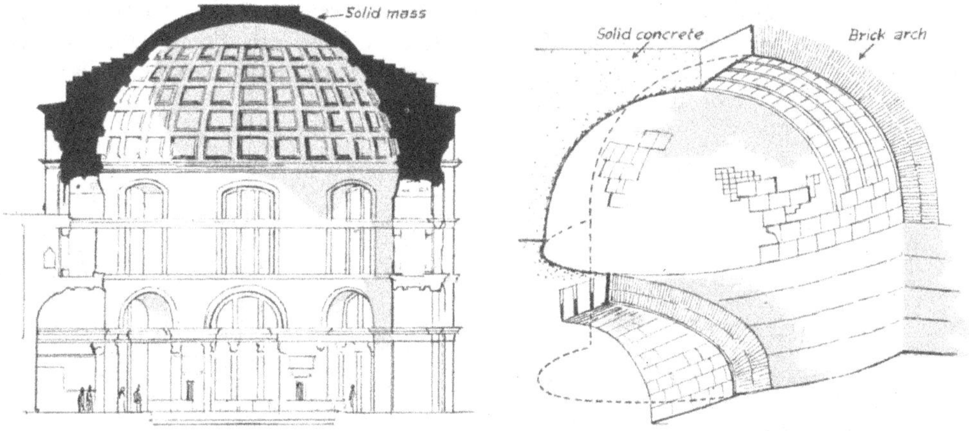

69 Roman construction: solid lids on circular spaces. (a) Semi-dome from the Baths of Caracella, Rome. (b) Section through a Calidarium.

enough water from the far-off hills. The Romans' answer was the arch.

With the arch and its logical development, the dome, the Romans could do everything they wanted to. They could build aqueducts and bridges that would last; great amphitheatres for sports and games, the back seats of which towered high above the ground and were reached by staircases leading up and through tiers of supporting arches; and public baths of a size hitherto quite unknown, in which the great spaces were covered by flat domes carried on immense arches.

In their temples the Romans continued the Greek traditions but on a bigger scale, because they could never quite resist the temptation to judge things by their size. As their Republic became an Empire and Romans penetrated the whole Mediterranean world and branched out to England and Germany and beyond, their culture declined.

But it is no use comparing it with Greek culture. It had a different purpose and served a mixed population governed by a mixture of grim-jowled soldiers, lawyers and luxurious financiers. It was a noble and impressive solution to the problem of empire building and sweetened the lives of a score of nations who reckoned themselves lucky to be counted citizens of Rome.

As this great Empire declined, it broke into parts. Sometimes one of these dominated the remainder, but in each part, so powerful was this dying giant, cities were built on a scale to match the parent city Rome, none greater or more magnificent than Constantinople, named after the Christian Emperor Constantine.

His largest architectural work was the Church of St Sophia, the real birthplace of the dome, which was never quite understood by the Romans, who built their domes by constructing a light shell of interlocking tiles filled over with a great thickness of concrete reinforced with lumps of stone. These relied upon their mass, therefore, and not on the interlocking tiles, and were not true domes.

The domes of St Sophia were light and thin and built up of small units each one of which transmitted the weight outwards and downwards, a true dome being in essence a series of arches arranged in a circle about a central point.

The church became a mosque when Constantinople fell under Mohammedan rule and the mosaics with which the domes and other surfaces were decorated were obliterated or destroyed. From what we can tell of smaller churches such as San Marco,

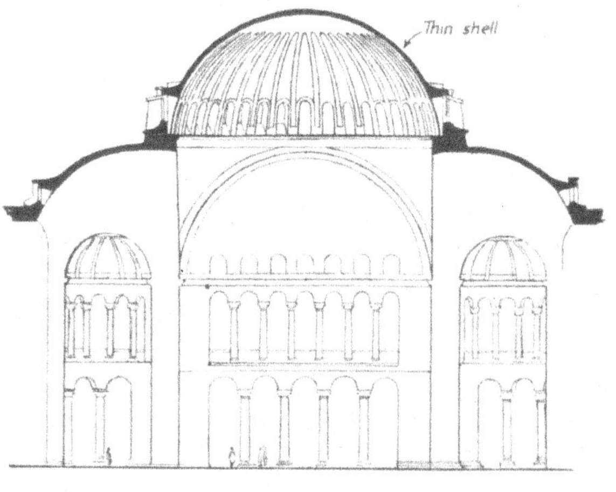

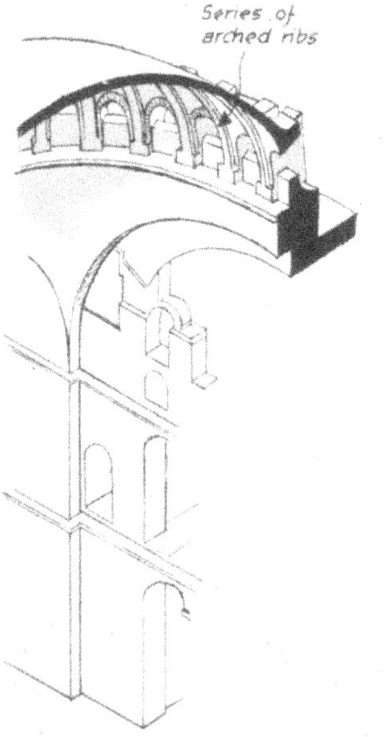

70 Byzantine construction: thin shells on arched ribs, covering great spaces.

Venice, or S. Vitale in Ravenna, another capital of the dying Empire, the effect must have been exquisite, as fine an interior space as man has ever conceived.

You may one day read the long sad story of the decay of the Roman Empire written by a rather stolid Englishman named Gibbon. He tells of the struggle to maintain the ancient virtues in the face of the temptation towards luxury and idleness offered by the steady stream of plunder and wealth flowing from every point of the compass into Rome; of the pollution of the jealously guarded Roman race and religion by foreigners from every land attracted or brought prisoner to it; of the growing discontent of the enormous slave population finding its first effective outlet in Christianity, the religion of submission and individual salvation; and of the slowly weakening efforts to withstand the pressure of wave upon wave of Asiatic and northern tribes in search of new living space.

The Empire finally broke up and vanished and the history of the next few centuries can be regarded as being a story of darkness and confusion or as the growth of the new light of Christianity. From now on Rome was a memory, preserved in the mighty ruins of its architecture, in the law of the Church and in the person of its Pope, so like the Emperor in his worldly and spiritual power. It was a memory that grew fainter as one part after another fell away into barbarism and chaos, and as war took the place of agriculture and trade as the chief and most honourable occupation of active men.

Of the glory that was past, only the Church remained, and for five or six centuries the growth of architecture is to be found entirely in church buildings – churches, monasteries and abbeys. But what a story this is, this slow transformation of a heavy imperial architecture into the spiritual and delicate loveliness of late Gothic tracery; and how lucky we are that so much of this story should have taken place in England.

In the early centuries the Church that had come to birth in the holes and corners of Rome, and in the catacombs below, was content to build in materials borrowed from the mounting dump of ruined splendour. The churches of Ravenna are no more than brick barns supported by old Roman columns and decorated with mosaics. But *what* mosaics! How they gleam and glow, as fresh now as though their workmen had left them but hours ago.

The masonic craft persisted, using the arch everywhere, but the dome only in the southern countries. The Church, conscious of its responsibilities, as the one rule of law and order in a warring world, and the single fountain of knowledge, stiffened into an organisation, based upon the Pope, and finally centred in Rome. Its creed and the order of its services, after arguments lasting some hundreds of years, became fixed in a ritual that separated the priesthood from the congregation and called for very particular types of building, long, narrow and in the form of a cross – no accident this!

There are in England a few examples of Saxon church buildings that carry the very faintest memory of the way the Romans used stone. Indeed, so mixed were the people in England when the Normans conquered it, that in an early Norman church at Kilpeck, near Hereford, the stone is used as though it were timber, and as though the designer was more used to building ships than churches. But in buildings going up all over Western Europe in the tenth and eleventh centuries – at which point we are going to take up the story – the semicircular arch and the massive column are the chief elements of building, and stone, which gave the impression of permanence and strength that a Church operating in a confused world was anxious to create, is its material.

The Church, you see, was re-colonising

71 Harlech Castle, one of a chain of castles built by Edward I to subdue the Welsh tribes. Its plan is a scientific response to the methods of warfare of the time.

the wasted Roman Empire, now overrun by a multitude of cheerful barbarians of unfixed habits and loose morals. Their seats of power were castles, whose great stone walls, which you can see in the older parts of the Tower of London, Rochester or in the famous Château Gaillard on the Seine, tell you clearly enough how dangerous life was for the brigand lords, and how doleful for the poor serfs. Scattered over the face of these troubled lands, like good deeds in a naughty world, were small colonies of priests living a life devoted to worship and the care of the poor, regulated by the strictest rules, and governed by superior priests holding their power direct from the Pope, and through him from God. In a world of war, plunder and misery, they alone offered forgiveness for sin and the hope of a life to come – two things of the utmost importance. Small wonder, then, that the Church should prosper and grow wealthy, should time and again purge itself of pride and loss of purpose, and send out into the world new waves of colonising priests, orders of Cistercians, Dominicans, Franciscans, each vowed to lives of useful sainthood and bound by stern rules of conduct.

It was for such communities that medieval architecture was developed, advancing with each fresh impulse to further understanding of the materials and structures with which the ecclesiastic life was housed and protected. It is the story of the stone arch carried to its logical conclusion, and beyond that, to collapse.

It is not necessary for you to know every step of this advance unless it particularly interests you, or to worry about the exact dates of each phase; these ancient buildings are there for you to admire and enjoy as part of your English inheritance rather than to trip you up in an examination. But the purpose of this architecture and the reasons why it should blossom as it did can be part of your enjoyment of it.

We have told you something of the role of the Church in the troublesome dark ages before the establishment of stability and the general rule of law. The original means of

72 The nave of Durham Cathedral: heavy columns and round arches in diminishing stages. Behind them a heavy wall with small windows.

building hark back to Italy, where in the churches we call Romanesque the arch was given a new significance as an element in building, replacing the solid wall by a wall of arches, diminishing in size as the wall rose: an economy of material and a move from darkness towards the light.

In the finest works of the Norman builders at Ely, Durham, Lincoln, Winchester, Rochester, etc., you will see the idea at work. First the line of massive columns, carrying firm stone arches; above this an arcade of smaller arches lit with windows; and above this, another carrying the screen of wall to the roof edge.

There are few roofs of stone built by Norman builders. It was an enormous undertaking and they fell back on timber as often as not. But this is how they did it.

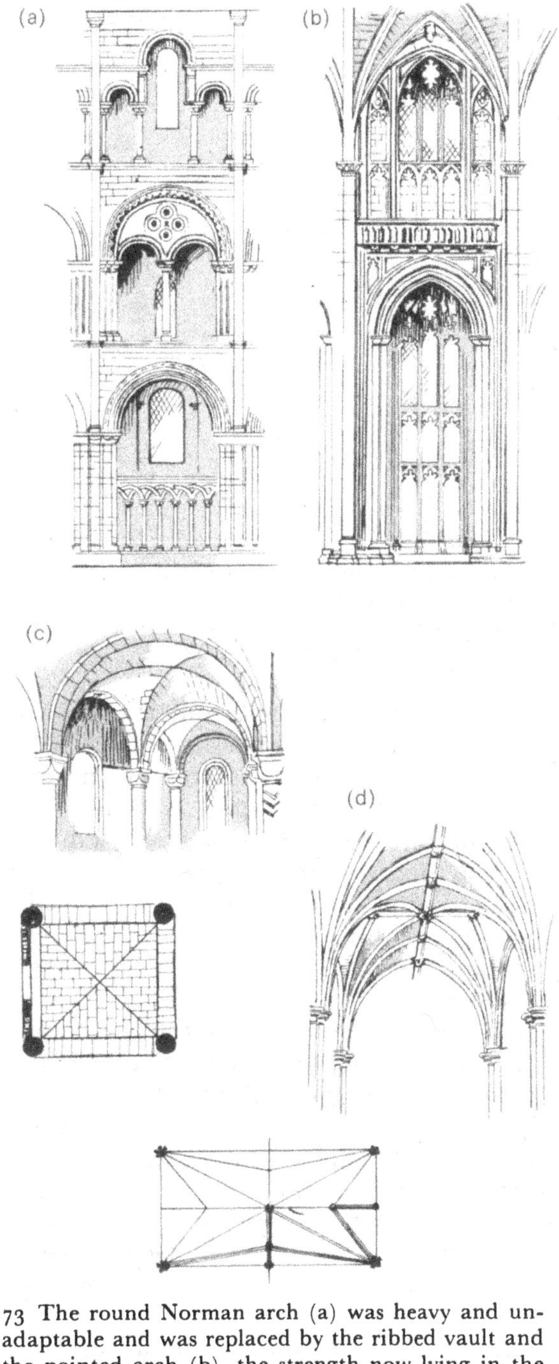

73 The round Norman arch (a) was heavy and unadaptable and was replaced by the ribbed vault and the pointed arch (b), the strength now lying in the stone rib with a lighter stone casing between. (c) Barrel vault, with plan. (d) Ribbed vaulting, with plan.

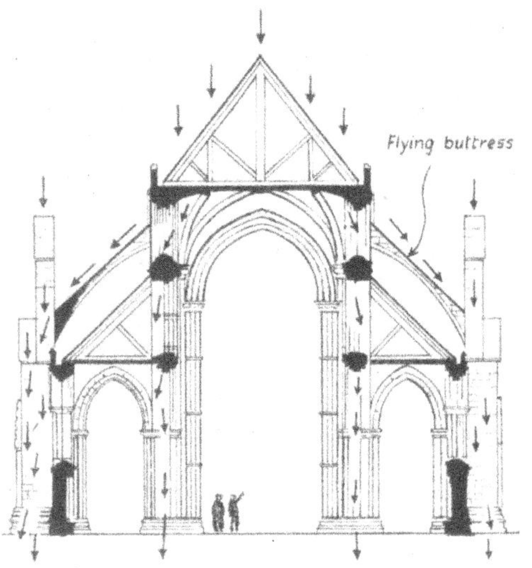

74 The logical engineering behind the imaginative design of great church building. The great weight of the roof carried out and pinned down by flying buttresses: a notable invention.

An arch when built is self-supporting. Two arches springing from opposite corners of a square plan make a sort of dome with four curved sections. Once the two arches are built, in big, carefully cut stones on an elaborate timber scaffolding rising from the pavement, the sides can be filled in with smaller and thinner stones, leaving the arch ribs standing out. The result is not a dome, but a vault.

The trouble about the semicircular Roman arch used by the Norman builders was its tendency to collapse under its own weight when not supported by surrounding walls, that is, when doing the most difficult job of roofing the nave of the church. This weakness, and the determination of the Church to build its house of God as permanently and as well as it knew how to, explain the next step forward.

Before we go forward, too, let us tell you that in its way, which was a massive and solid way, Norman architecture was as beautiful as anything that came after, with a rough kind of geometric ornament exactly suited to its character.

The attempt to achieve permanence in stone, and thereby to avoid the medieval man's constant fear of fire, was rewarded by an entirely successful invention. This consisted of a pointed arch that overcame any tendency towards collapse, and the flying buttress, by means of which the weight or thrust of this arch was carried to the ground without the necessity for the heavy wall used by Norman builders for this purpose. With this double invention the church builders overcame their worst troubles, and at once their architecture took on a new character, the one by which it is most easily recognised. In place of the massive stone drum and the heavy wall pierced by tiny windows, we now have slim shafts of stonework rising to the lofty vaults of the aisles and nave, and between this stone framework areas of coloured glass that tell the story of the Bible and the history of the Church in the most beautiful way ever imagined.

After the effort of thought, the scientific problem of support having yielded an answer at last, the architecture burst into full flower, never more flower-like than in its early stages, known to us as Early English.

The columns are now no more than clusters of thin stems bound together at intervals, rising upward, branching off to support lower levels of covered space, but sending members upward again to the intricate branchwork of the roof, the supreme test of these master builders. What might be a dim forest assembly of shadows, when lit by the rosy grandeur of the story windows becomes a joyful hymn of praise, a hymn in which the smallest part joins, for now the means of building are secure it is time to decorate whatever is proper for decoration. At every junction of rib or shaft there sprouted the decorations that, drawn from

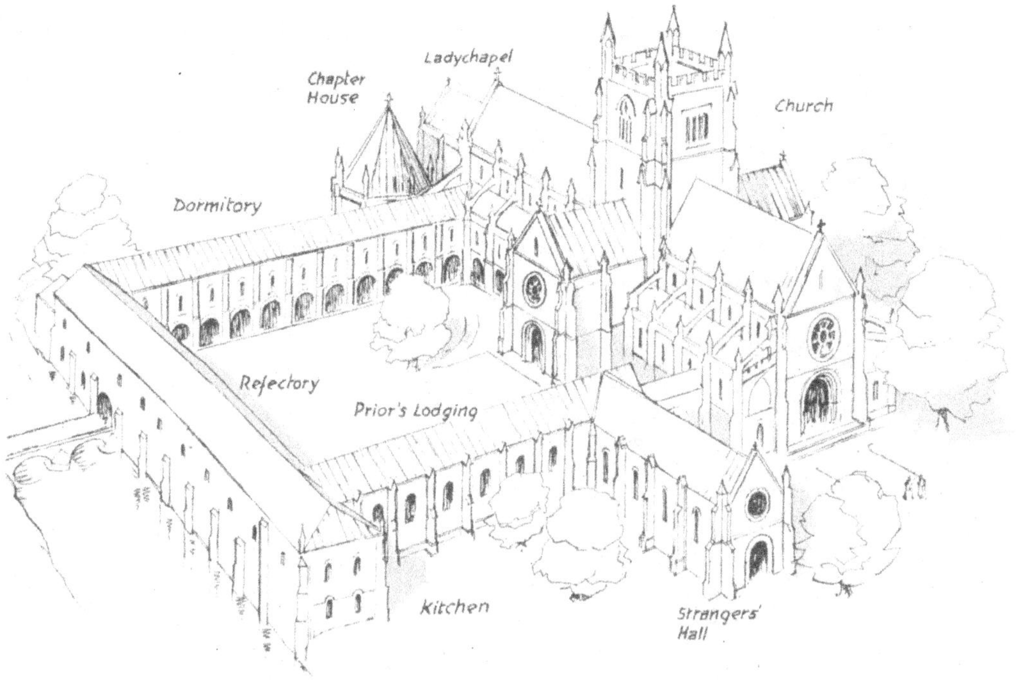

75 The intellectual centre of medieval life: a monastic building in which God was glorified, knowledge preserved, and the affairs of the world administered.

the foliage and flower life of our native country, have so endeared the medieval churchman to us.

Do not imagine that these lovely decorations were carved in joyful abandon by any workman who had a fancy for it; or that these churches and cathedrals were the work of men who dispensed with an architect because they were so moved by beauty. In actual fact, our modern architecture is not as strictly ordered as this, nor does it exceed it in mathematical daring or technical skill. It is most certain that the ornament was most carefully placed to emphasise the beauty of the whole structure, and funny faces under choir stalls are a good joke, but not very important after all.

No, what is so striking about medieval architecture is its extreme originality of thought and purpose – originality in its proper sense of something that springs from the origin of the matter and owes its form to direct personal revelation or experience. In Early English architecture there is no trace of Rome: it is as new as, compared with our immediate architectural past, modern architecture is new.

In our opinion, Early English is architecture at its best: it was never more beautiful again. Yet it could still change and develop, and before it died it produced one final invention in the form of fan vaulting. This is no more than the pointed arch vault multiplied until its many ribs, like the veins of some supporting leaf form, make an uninterrupted spreading surface of roof. It is a very lovely and delicate fancy, as you may see for yourself in King Henry VII's Chapel at Westminster, Eton Chapel, or that masterpiece of royal munificence, King's

76 King's College Chape
Cambridge. The ultimate glor
of English church architecture
the logical outcome crowne
with the beauty of fan vaultin
and stained glass.

College Chapel, Cambridge.

When a king replaces church and people as chief church builder, it is time to say farewell. With Henry VIII church building ends suddenly and tragically, having bequeathed to laymen a heritage of actual buildings and a native skill that you may admire in many a village, in barns, and in the entirely new palace-houses of the Elizabethan wool barons and aristocrats, which replaced the grim castles of former ages.

But there was no real life left in medievalism. The air was full of new thoughts and new purposes and a new age of world discovery and overseas trade was being born.

Italy, fortunate in lying at the meeting of trade routes from all over Europe to the East, once more provided the impetus to the new valuation of life. Medieval life was feudal and communal. This new life was individual and commercial. Freed from the need for common worship and communal

77 Castle turning into house: Stokesay Castle, Shropshire, built for a wool financier at the time of Edward I.

society, it set about finding new standards of thought and action, and found them in Rome, in the ancient Rome that had become only a memory.

The Renaissance, or rebirth, was a going back in that it was a return to a classic outlook developed so long ago, but in fact it was a liberation from the narrow doctrines of a Church that had said all it had to say to humanity. Men felt the need to think for themselves again, and to enjoy and make the best of this life rather than the next. In the poetry and philosophy of the Romans, but above all in their architecture and sculpture, these active men of the Renaissance found their means of expression, and in the space of a few years had transformed it into a new thing, their own. The ancient streams of Greek and Roman thought had flowed again to fertilise a new and vigorous life, springing from the original Mediterranean stem.

When England awoke to the situation, the Renaissance in Italy and France was beginning to exhaust itself, and had already built its finest buildings, painted its most famous pictures, and written its most lasting poems. But coming last to the feast we stayed longest, and so made up a little for our remoteness from the source of new life.

The Reformation was the first sign of change in England, but it was the discovery of the new world in which we took a prominent share that placed us, though we did not know it, at the centre of the world, and prepared us for greater power to come: economics dictated the need for individual conscience, and an individual conscience meant freedom of individual action.

From now on you are to imagine England as dominated by trade and commerce and swayed in its actions by the ideas of the ancient Romans, who valued the art of living,

78 The end of medieval architecture. Renaissance fancy grafted on to an old plant. Hatfield House, Hertfordshire.

79 The market hall in a grand seventeenth-century dress. Abingdon Town Hall, built in 1677.

respected law and order and a just proportion in everything, in manners as in art and architecture. Medievalism was as dead as the dodo.

The very first traces of classical architecture in England are to be met with in the extravagant carvings of Elizabethan houses, quaint cherubs and oddly proportioned columns that came to us from Holland. Henry VII's tomb in Westminster Abbey is, by an accident, the work of an Italian, but our first intimations of novelty came at second hand. Inigo Jones, designer of masque settings and architecture to the Court of Charles I, brought back from Italy his experiences of a later form of Renaissance named after its principal exponent, Palladio. He built the Banqueting Hall in Whitehall which was intended to be part of a magnificent palace for his unlucky King; and there it is today, a most stirring example of Palladian architecture. He also built several country houses, a type of building that the English were to develop into something quite their own.

In the next two centuries – the seventeenth and the eighteenth – we used the classical vernacular as though it were our own, and made it an instrument of a culture of very high order, an aristocratic rather than a communal culture, but no less perfect in itself for that.

We were growing gradually but steadily richer; the classic idea suited us exactly; society, though savagely divided into rich and poor, was stable, and everything was set for a period of slow assimilation of ideas as they came, and a gradual enrichment of thought. This is the condition most favourable to the perfection of an art, and we are fortunate that so great a part of our towns and so many buildings of importance were built under its influence.

The early part of this period is dominated by the giant figure of Sir Christopher Wren, who outlived his youthful fame as a scientist and mathematician to become the greatest architect our country has produced. The Fire of London, which destroyed much of the medieval city, gave him the opportunity of building a large cathedral and a whole range of buildings, and of creating a new architecture suited to the English.

You probably know how well he succeeded and that St Paul's Cathedral, Chelsea and Greenwich Hospitals, Hampton Court and his City churches are among our most precious national possessions. You may not realise what we owe to his creation of a definite manner of domestic building – simple brick-built houses with white painted sash windows, canopied door, tile roof hidden behind parapets, arranged in series round a square that is reminiscent of the medieval cloister but is in fact a much freer institution. With this as a model we began to build towns on a scale and size that matched our growing prosperity and rising population.

Why did this classicism suit us so well? First, because we had emerged from medievalism towards an age of reason and inquiry and could enjoy the ancient culture again; second, because classical architecture responded to our feelings of release by giving us space, and to our wealthy man's sense of importance and responsibility by lodging him in a temple fitted with the conveniences of domesticity or business; and it was essentially a noble way of building.

Its materials were brick and stone, timber of oak and pine, and later, deal from Russia; wrought iron and lead, for both use and ornament; tiles and slate; glass; and paint for woodwork both inside and out. These materials sufficed for all the needs of building, and though some of them, like glass, were improved upon in the course of time, and though painted stucco provided an elegant but cheap substitute for stone for the benefit of the bourgeois classes of the late eighteenth and very early nineteenth centuries, they remained unaltered for close upon 200 years, and enabled the architecture to purify and refine itself.

As a result the design and making of nearly everything, from great buildings down to knives and forks, the merely useful as well as the ornamental, were impregnated by the classic spirit and distinguished by the purity, elegance and confidence of a completely realised culture.

As one might expect of an architecture so well understood, its sphere of influence was expended to include the design of whole districts and even whole towns. Bath is much the most famous of these, though there are many other fine examples, such as the West End of London (Nash), New Town, Edinburgh (Playfair), Dublin, Cheltenham and Buxton.

In 1820 this architecture held sway. By 1850 it was gone, swept away by the onrush of an industrialism of which the causes could be traced to the colonisation of the new world and the East and to the growth of science – so actively pursued by Christopher Wren and his contemporaries – which in the nineteenth century accelerated and led to the discovery of steam power for industry and transport. The population of the country trebled, but in quantity only, the bulk of the additions being the illiterate wage-slaves of industry, living lives of ignorance and misery in towns hastily run up to house them without benefit of sanitation, or any decency, social, medical or aesthetic.

You may have noticed how slowly the architecture of Greece and Rome, the Middle Ages and the Renaissance developed. The first signs of the English Renaissance are to be found in Elizabeth's reign. It begins to be understood in Charles I's reign, and produces a few good buildings. Under Charles II it flowers into the work of Wren and his contemporaries, goes on to refine itself through reigns of kings and queens, and is still alive and flourishing well into the Regency. There must be time to assimilate and digest, to experiment, to learn by trial and error, to understand wholly; time thereafter for the confident expression of life, the last aim of architecture.

The Victorians above all things lacked time. They were conscious of the fact but thought that it could be made up for by machinery. They were wrong. Georgian architecture lost its master and degenerated to the grossness of Victorianism. The architecture of engineering became the one really living art form, though it found its outlet through works of pure utility such as bridges, railway locomotives, station roofs and the like. Meanwhile architecture, because it was unable to find a purpose among this new disjointed society, or to recognise iron, steel and machinery as being its materials, floundered about aimlessly, a prey to the rich classes who saw in it no more than the means of registering their newly acquired social rank.

When original ideas are not to be had, second-hand ones must do. There is no other explanation for the architectural revivals that succeeded one another during the nineteenth and early twentieth centuries and turned architects, who should be the prime wardens of a nation's culture, into shopmen willing, for money, to provide any style out of an extensive repertory ranging over the whole history of architecture.

The beginning of this century showed us the results of a century of unplanning. Unrestrained industrialism accompanied by great increases in the numbers of poorly educated people had produced conditions of squalor over vast areas. The towns, already cut up by railways, were slum-ridden and spread out in ribbon formation along the roads into the country.

Architecture, which had grudgingly

80 The Houses of Parliament. A true nineteenth-century mixture. Designed by a classically-minded architect, and decorated in the Gothic style, it is a noble monument to the genius of its time.

accepted the new factory-made materials, components and machines tried to hide them behind facades of various styles: Gothic for colleges, classic for banks, something like Egyptian for factories on the Great West Road.

Towards the middle of the century, on the initiative of John Ruskin and William Morris, there was a revolt against philistinism from which issued on the one hand the abortive Pre-Raphaelite movement in painting, and on the other a return of the Middle Ages in architecture which had a more positive aspect.

Though public and monumental Gothic architecture petered out in dry scholarship, domestic architecture led directly to the garden village idea that was the cradle of town and country planning. Hampstead Garden Suburb provided the models for an informal house built honestly of good materials, in an informal cosy sort of manner that suited the emerging lower-middle classes. The garden city plan swept both classical formality and industrial rigidity away completely.

Ebenezer Howard then applied these ideas to the problem of a too rapidly expanding London in the form of a self-contained city surrounded by a protective green belt, and built Letchworth in Hertfordshire as the first of all the New Towns. The New Town movement that followed the last war was Howard's positive contribution; and the endless suburbs of semi-detached villas was industry's negative response to him, for in an over-industrialised country like ours it never rains but it pours!

We cannot go forward for ever looking backward and it was inevitable that architects should come to grips with industrialism in an attempt to harmonise its materials and methods with the creative principles of art.

The modern movement in architecture was the climax of a number of sporadic movements on the Continent and in America, which came to a head before the war in Germany under the leadership of Walter Gropius, Mies van der Rohe and Le Corbusier, whose works and buildings influenced the whole world of architecture.

Much of this book is concerned with the theory and practices of the modern movement, and many of the examples illustrated are by its members and followers. The modern movement continues to provide the only true basis for an architecture in tune with the dominant productive system of our time, and if it is in doubt it is only because the whole system upon which it depends is under fire from those who see this system as the cause of overcrowding, depersonalisation and pollution. Clearly these evils remain with us, and can only be dispersed by the generations that read this book.

Glossary

Aluminium A white soft metal that does not tarnish easily.
Arcade A continuous open passage.
Asphalt A smooth, hard, brown or blackish mineral sometimes found in lakes, used in making roads and pavements.
Capital The top of a column or pillar, usually moulded.
Cornice A horizontal moulded projection on top of a building or some part of a building; sometimes a moulding that runs around the top of a room.
Dome A rounded form, usually semi-circular in all directions except the base, which is round. Often used on the roof of a building or part of it.
Duct A channel or tube, either round or rectangular, used for conveying water, electricity etc. in a building.
Flying Buttress A support for a pier or vertical member in a building springing from the top of the member and going at an angle down to the ground, usually carried by a segment of an arch. Its purpose is to resist the thrust of the roof or floor and to carry the weight down to the ground.
Lintel A member spanning an opening, transferring the weight of material above to walls on either side of the opening.
Mortice A cavity or hole into which the end of some other part of a lock or frame is fitted to form a joint. In carpentry, it is the counterpart of a tenon.
Perspex A translucent form of plastic.
Reinforced Concrete Concrete made stronger by the insertion of steel rods for use in columns, beams and floors etc.
Relief Three-dimensional work.
Tenon The projecting member of timber or steel, usually timber, which goes into the mortice to make a joint.
Wattle and Daub An old method of building in which earth was condensed by pounding with water and reinforced with straw or sticks or any other handy material to make walls. Probably the oldest form of building known and still much in use among primitive peoples.

Index